Praise for *How to Blog a Book*

Recycling your blog posts into a book may provide the easiest way to write a book, and *How to Blog a Book* provides the plan for producing both the blog and a book that agents, publishers, and readers will notice.

> **DAN POYNTER,** author of *The Self-Publishing Manual* and *How to Write Nonfiction*. www.parapublishing.com

If you've been thinking about writing a book, Nina Amir removes the barriers to getting it done and provides you with a formula for making it easy. Who doesn't love easy? This book should give birth to a lot of new books, and if you read it, one of those books could be YOURS!

> **STEPHANIE CHANDLER,** author of *The Writer's Guide to Building an Online Platform*. www.authoritypublishing.com

Blogging is a great way to create content for a book. Nina has put together a road map for getting a book out of your blog posts. Check out *How to Blog a Book*. It covers all the stops along the way to your destination as a published author.

> **JOHN KREMER,** author of *1001 Ways to Market Your Book*. www.bookmarket.com

The old saying "kill two birds with one stone" is the perfect metaphor for what Nina teaches in this valuable book. Blogging with the intention of turning the accumulated material into a complete trade book is a brilliant concept.

> **JEFF HERMAN,** literary agent. www.jeffherman.com

Today writers have to think outside the box when it comes to getting their book ideas published. Blogging a book offers a unique way not only to attract readers but to catch the eyes of acquisitions editors—just what every aspiring author wants and needs to sell books.

> **JILL LUBLIN,** co-author of *Guerrilla Publicity* and author of *Get Noticed, Get Referrals* and *Networking Magic*. www.jilllublin.com

Nina Amir's new book is a book writing and promotion revelation. She shows you how to finish your manuscript at the same time as you build a platform. Every writer will benefit from reading this slender, savvy volume.

> **RICK FRISHMAN,** best-selling author, publisher, and speaker. www.rickfrishman.com

At the turn of the twenty-first century, everyone began to realize they needed a blog. To-day, people realize they need a book, too. Why not do both at the same time? Nina helps you understand how to easily write a book and build a platform.

JIM F. KUKRAL, author of *Business Around a Lifestyle* and five other titles. www.digitalbooklaunch.com

Turning your blog posts into a book is a terrific way to write your book and build your audience at the same time. Nina Amir will guide you through every step with practical advice based on real-world experience.

DANA LYNN SMITH, author of the *Savvy Book Marketer* series of marketing guides for authors. www.savvybookmarketer.com

There's a lot more involved in creating a book out of a blog than just gathering up a bunch of posts and hitting "publish." Nina Amir leads you step-by-step through all the consideration. Say good-bye to "what should I write about?" and say hello to "I'm a published author."

SHEL HOROWITZ, book shepherd and award-winning author of eight books including *Guerrilla Marketing Goes Green* and *Grassroots Marketing for Authors and Publishers*. www.frugalmarketing.com

I believe that blogging can change your life. I also believe that writing a book is one of the achievements you will be most proud of. Combining the two can be a brilliant way to get the project moving. Nina's book will help you organize the process so you can put all your time and energy into writing and building a community.

JOANNA PENN, author and blogger at The Creative Penn, voted one of the Top 10 Blogs for Writers. www.thecreativepenn.com

Nina demonstrates a simplified writing process that supports both the final manuscript production and an author's long-term marketing goals.

BRADLEY FLORA, Executive Director, www.SPANnet.org

If you are just starting out as a blogger or if you already have 15,000 posts online, Nina Amir's *How to Blog a Book* has the plan for you. You can't go wrong with this book. Written to provide you with the easiest path from screen to page, *How to Blog a Book* gets you there while helping you to dodge pitfalls and common frustrations. Read it and learn.

SHANE BIRLEY, co-author of *Blogging for Dummies*. www.shanesworld.ca

http://howtoblogabook.com

HOW TO
BLOG
A BOOK

WD
WRITER'S DIGEST
BOOKS

WritersDigest.*com*
Cincinnati, Ohio

write, publish, and promote your work one post at a time

NINA AMIR
Forewords by Christina Katz and Chris Garrett

For more resources for writers, visit www.writersdigest.com/books.

To receive a free weekly e-mail newsletter delivering tips and updates about writing and about Writer's Digest products, register directly at http://newsletters.fwpublications.com.

15 14   5 4 3

Distributed in Canada by Fraser Direct
100 Armstrong Avenue
Georgetown, Ontario, Canada L7G 5S4
Tel: (905) 877-4411

Distributed in the U.K. and Europe by F&W Media International
Brunel House, Newton Abbot, Devon, TQ12 4PU, England
Tel: (+44) 1626-323200, Fax: (+44) 1626-323319
E-mail: postmaster@davidandcharles.co.uk

Distributed in Australia by Capricorn Link
P.O. Box 704, Windsor, NSW 2756 Australia
Tel: (02) 4577-3555

Edited by Melissa Wuske
Designed by Claudean Wheeler
Production coordinated by Debbie Thomas

DEDICATION

To all *aspiring* authors who would like to become *published* authors.

And to the late Professor John Keats, who said, "If you can write an article, you can write a nonfiction book. A nonfiction book is just a series of articles on the same topic strung together." I strung a series of related blog posts together instead. I hope you're proud, JK.

ACKNOWLEDGMENTS

I'd like to thank, first, Michael Larsen and Elizabeth Pomada for including me as a panelist at the San Francisco Writers Conference. From that opportunity the *How to Blog a Book* blog was born. Second, my webmaster and blogmaster Linda Lee offered support and counsel. Third, my agent, Verna Dreisbach, saw the entire "me" and a path to help me succeed.

Shane Birley, Linda Lee, and Bill Belew served as consultants on the chapters containing technical information, reading chapters several times. Sue Collier also lent her expertise to the section on self-publishing.

At Writer's Digest Books, I'd like to thank Phil Sexton, Kelly Messerly, Melissa Wuske, Kim Catanzarite, Roseann S. Biederman, Michael Scott Francis, Claudean Wheeler, Rachael Smith, Debbie Thomas, Stacy Heyderhoff, and Nicole Miller for supporting all my editorial, design, marketing, and promotion needs.

I'd also like to thank my blog readers, who helped me to become a published author. In particular, I'd like to thank my husband, Ron—once upon a time my only blog reader. Every blogger needs a first reader. And every writer needs a supporter, an advocate, and a listening ear. Ron has been all that and more.

I want to thank my mother for encouraging my creative bent for all these years. Here's a book that's not *bubkes*, Mom!

Last, but not least, huge heaps of gratitude to Karen Stone, my best friend. If I couldn't have shared this journey with you, it would have been awfully lonely.

http://howtoblogabook.com

CONTENTS

FOREWORD

By Christina Katz

Can literary excellence be achieved via blogging? Can you actually blog your way to long-term publishing success? I don't see why not. However, it's up to the writer who is blogging to elevate a pedestrian practice anyone can attempt into an inspired journey that results in a masterful book.

The possibility of blogging a book reaffirms my conviction that there has never been a better time to be a writer. I share this perspective with a number of folks in the extended writing community including Nina Amir, who has authored this friendly, step-by-step guide on how to blog your way to a book.

In the past, writers had two choices: traditional publishing or "indie-publishing." Today, publishing happens on a spectrum and more publishing options become available every day. The necessity of choosing *us* or *them* is over. We are now better off pursuing all of our options to the best of our abilities. Every writer is a publisher. What once applied to some is now a fact for all. And the onus is on each writer to weigh the pros and cons of every professional choice we make, to partner wisely with other professionals, and to produce our own long-term career success.

Above all, remember this: The needs of the reader always trump a writer's ambitions, obsessions, and predilections. Readers are less patient than ever. Therefore writers of any genre must consistently sweat it out until art enters into the equation.

This is where Nina Amir's book comes to your writing-for-publication rescue. She can help you with the inspiration and the mechanics of getting your blog-to-book started. The tools in this book will help you get started. The inspirational interviews will help you finish what you dare to begin. The nitty-gritty covered herein will help you take care of business.

Once you've read this book, it's up to you to put your highest quality effort into your work. I wish you the best of luck using blogging to bring out the best in your writing. I am sure you will not settle for anything less. And then your readers will thank you.

FOREWORD
by Chris Garrett

When I started blogging, not only was there no name for the process, but there wasn't really any aim to it, either. There were, of course, people who suggested that we were creating a whole new world, that somehow we were building the future one "HTML tag" at a time.

Years ago if you wanted to reach an audience online you had to learn some pretty complicated things (such as geek-speak like that "HTML tag" phrase from the previous paragraph). Now, with modern blogging tools, anyone can publish their thoughts online with relative ease.

In the early days, most of us just shared whatever was on our minds at the time, which could be anything from inspired or innovative to mundane. As I write this, blogging has matured. It might not be quite "grown up," but we have come a long way from that humble beginning to now. A blog has come to mean more than just an online public journal; it's also a powerful tool for creating content and building an audience.

While some blogs are still online diaries, there are also many successful online magazines, storefronts, galleries, and web comics. A blog can be used to brainstorm, discuss topics, and gather your thoughts.

You might want to write a book based on the topic of your blog or repurpose the content you created for your blog into a book.

Today there is a tremendous opportunity for bloggers to become authors. Nina will help you learn to use these blogging tools to generate ideas, create and structure content, and compile entire books. She will share strategies to help you avoid making the same mistakes as the blogging pioneers.

The audience you attract with your blog might even help you find a publisher for your book.

Of course, not every blogger will be "discovered" and find fame and fortune, but as a blogger armed with Nina's advice, you will be in much better shape to *finish* your book, and that's more than most people can say!

INTRODUCTION

WHY I STARTED A BLOG
ABOUT HOW TO BLOG A BOOK

In January of 2009 I started a blog about how to blog a book. At that time I had way too many nonfiction book projects started and not finished—at least seven or eight. Though my expertise lies in nonfiction books, I also had one novel manuscript tucked away in a file on my computer.

So why would I start a blog that would force me to begin writing another book? Why would I want to write a book in the public eye, where anyone could see whether I made progress and whether I finished it and what my rough draft looked like?

I did it because blogging a book represents a great idea. Not only does blogging offer one of the quickest and easiest ways to write a book, blogging technology provides aspiring authors with the ability to promote themselves and their books as they write. This means writers build a following of blog readers as they blog their books into existence—a following of readers who also will buy a printed book based upon those very same blog posts.

Why not simply write a book the old-fashioned way and traditionally or independently publish it instead? Today writers have to become more creative if they want to produce successful books; i.e., books that sell to readers and to publishers. They have to take their careers into their own hands. They have to become their own public relations representatives, and promotion and marketing directors. They have to start their own publishing companies. Taking advantage of the current online technology allows authors to do these things easily and inexpensively, if not effortlessly.

We live in the Internet Age. Many people spend much of their day connected to the World Wide Web. They also read online.

While other forms of publishing cost money, blogging your book is free—or can be. You can begin blogging and "publish" your book one post at a time on the Internet for nothing. Zero. Zilch. Or next to zilch, if you so choose.

Plus, if you write good copy and promote your blog well, it's possible to gain more readers than you would with a traditionally published book. Imagine one hundred, one thousand, ten thousand, or even one hundred thousand people a day reading your blog. Wouldn't you find that rewarding? Wouldn't you find it exciting? Wouldn't you feel successful as an author?

Blogs constitute one of the best ways today to build the coveted writer's platform. A blog read by thousands of people each month goes a long way toward impressing a publisher or selling your independently published book. In fact, many publishers now expect aspiring authors to have blogs and to blog often. It behooves aspiring authors, therefore, to become bloggers.

CHAPTER 1:

BOOK BLOGGING BASICS

As you read this book, agents and acquisitions editors are scanning the Internet to find new writers with great ideas to turn into books. Where do they find them? In the blogosphere, that place where bloggers write and blogs are published, read, and commented upon.

Research done by *Publishers Marketplace* estimates that more than fifty blogs landed book deals in 2009 alone—some other industry experts say sixty. However, the database produced by *Publishers Marketplace*, a publication that provides membership information for publishing professionals, included only *announced* deals. We can safely assume that if announced and unannounced deals were added together for that time period, the total number of contracts handed out by publishers to bloggers might be much larger. Although 2009 marked the height of the blog-to-book craze, the blog-to-book trend has continued. *Publishers Marketplace* has released no new statistics for the years following the first burst that occurred from about 2003 to 2009, but a steady flow of blog-to-book success stories continues to surface. I estimate that about six books were released each month in 2011, which would make that year hotter for blog-to-book deals than 2009. Here are just a few recent blog-to-book titles:

- Reggie Solomon's *I Garden: Urban Style* (based on his blog by the same name) was released by Betterway Books in December 2010.
- Neil Pasricha's *The Book of Awesome* (based on his blog 1,000 Awesome Things) was published by Berkley Trade in April 2010.

- Martha Alderson's *The Plot Whisperer* (based on her blog by the same name) was released by Adams Media in October 2011.
- Jill Smokler's *Confessions of a Scary Mommy* (based on her blog Scary Mommy) will be released by Simon & Schuster in time for Mother's Day 2012 .

Some of the writers who landed these contracts simply blogged their way to a deal; some of them blogged actual books. In both cases, they turned out copy that attracted readers' and publishers' attention, and they did it one post at a time.

How can you, too, accomplish this feat? How can you become the next big blog-to-book success story? You can do so by writing and publishing a successful book—one that gets noticed by readers and publishers—in cyberspace. You can do so by not only writing your book using blog technology, but by successfully promoting it on the Internet so you build an author's platform, a fan base or readership, large enough to impress any literary agent or acquisitions editor at a publishing house.

WHAT'S A BLOG, ANYWAY?

Many writers know little about blogging or refuse to learn. When you purchased this book, you placed yourself among those aspiring authors ready and willing to embrace the technology of twenty-first-century publishing. Congratulations! By doing so, you took an important first step toward getting ahead of your competition and meeting your writing and publishing goals as well.

Since you are considering blogging a book, I'll assume you know what a blog is. You may never have bothered to research the origins of the word *blog*, though. So, let's start there. The word *blog* represents a contraction of "web log," which is a shared online journal in which a person can post diary entries about her personal experiences or hobbies. At least, that's how blogs began. Once upon a time, people thought of blogs as places to share their streams of consciousness. Now blogs tend to be much more targeted and directed at particular audiences and subject matter. Bloggers pick a topic, often in a niche, about which to write.

Typically a blog is written and edited by an individual *blogger* (noun). *To blog* (verb) means to write or edit a shared online journal and to add *posts*, or content, to the blog. Some bloggers hire ghostwriters or use *guest bloggers* (posts from experts or other bloggers). *Blog maintenance* entails publishing posts to the Internet and taking care of updating the blogging program and its features. Some bloggers hire experts to design or maintain their blogs for them.

While bloggers may write about personal experiences, business, news, politics, hobbies, sports, health, opinions, or just about anything else, blogs are anything but personal in the sense that bloggers publish them in cyberspace for anyone and everyone to read. There's nothing personal about that; in fact, writing a blog is about as public as you can get. You may choose to write about a personal topic, but you'll do it publicly.

Many blogs offer commentary on a particular subject, cover various aspects of the news, or offer expert advice on a particular subject. Blogs often combine text with images, include audio and video, and provide links to other similar blogs, websites, and online resources. Readers also can comment on posts, an aspect of blogs that makes them interactive.

A blog also constitutes a type of website. For writers who may not feel capable of managing a website, a blog provides a way to have an online presence that is manageable by even the least tech savvy of people. I consider blogs website solutions for the technologically handicapped.

WHO CAN BLOG?

Anyone can blog or become a blogger. No one and nothing stops you from opening a free (yes, free) account with a site like WordPress.com, Blogger.com, or TypePad.com, and beginning to blog.

If you want a self-hosted blog (more on this in chapter five), you may need some help. If you are technologically adept, you can manage this yourself. A self-hosted blog does cost a little bit of money, but not much. You will need to pay for a domain name and a hosting account. I recommend a self-hosted blog for your blogged book; I'll explain why in chapter five.

WHO CAN BLOG A BOOK?

While it's true that anyone can become a blogger (but not necessarily a *successful* blogger), not anyone can blog a book. To blog a whole book you must have the ability to write a book from start to finish. This entails conceptualizing a complete book, organizing the book, and carrying out the concept from the first to the last page—in this case in short, targeted posts written on a regular basis—and publishing it on the Internet.

Anyone who can write and has writing worth reading can blog. (Actually lots of people who have little to write about and no writing worth reading have blogs, blog, and call themselves bloggers.) However, the same rules apply to blogging a book as to writing any other nonfiction book (or work of fiction for that matter). After all, even though you are composing your book post by post in cyberspace, you still are writing a book.

- You must have a great, saleable idea with a big enough market to make it worth writing.
- You need to have enough information to fill a book (a minimum of 25,000-30,000 words, which is an 80- to 100-page book). In most cases, you'll need to fill significantly more pages than that to satisfy a publisher.
- You need to be—or to become—the expert on your topic. In some cases, you can gain expert status by blogging and blogging well—an added advantage of blogging. The more great content you provide over time, the higher likelihood you have of being perceived as an authority on your subject. (How do you think I became the expert on how to blog a book?)
- Your blogged book must offer value to readers.

If you and your subject matter meet all these criteria, you are ready and able to blog a book. If you don't, you can still blog. You just may not want to blog a book.

In fact, some people who have been blogging for a while with no intention of writing a book later decide they do, indeed, want to turn their blogs into books. The majority of blog-to-book success stories come from bloggers discovered by publishers because of their great blogs; they then had to mine a year or several years of blog posts for those that would best fit into a book. This is most often called *recycling* or *repurposing* your blog posts into a book. Author and book designer Joel Friedlander, however, coined the term "booking a blog," which I like to use instead. It's the reverse of blogging a book. When you book a blog you don't plan on writing a book via your blog, but later recycle posts into a printed book; when you blog a book, you preplan your book and your posts so you produce a manuscript for the express purpose of producing a digital or printed book.

That leads me to the next question: What subjects can (or should) you blog about?

WHAT SUBJECTS CAN I BLOG OR BLOG A BOOK ABOUT?

Some industry experts estimate that the number of "active" English-language combined with non-English blogs might have reached over one billion in 2010, although I've never seen statistics to support this fact. More specifically, as of mid-December 2010, Technorati.com, an Internet search engine for locating English-language blogs (also known as a blog aggregator), had indexed 1,288,726 such blogs.

The difference in these statistics isn't important—nor is the accuracy of the first estimate. Here's the point: Each one of those blogs represents a subject. That means you can blog about just about anything.

This fact raises another question: Should a blogger choose any subject for a blogged book? No.

Technically a blogger can, indeed, choose any topic. No blogging police will pull your blog off the Internet if the subject you choose for your blogged book is stupid or boring, for example. No written rules say, "You can only blog books on these particular topics."

However, some blog subjects simply don't lend themselves to books. Some blog subjects have too small a market. In other words, they won't generate enough readers to make blogging a book worthwhile. Typically, the larger the market for your book, the better.

That said, sometimes picking a subject that targets a specific small market can be good. Big markets can be difficult to penetrate, especially if a lot of other bloggers or authors are doing a good job with them already. Niche markets can prove quite profitable.

I once wanted to write a book about the Jewish Sabbath. One publisher asked me to re-angle it to include all religions that celebrate the Sabbath. This would have given the book a larger market and made it more saleable in that publisher's eyes. An agent, however, asked me to change, or hone, the topic so it narrowed that same book's market to only Jewish women. She felt the book would sell better—to a publisher and to readers—if the market was smaller and more focused.

Some blog subjects are too personal for a book, such as the blog my physical therapist started so he could share photos and news about his newborn baby. Some blogs aren't written in a style that lends itself to printed-book form. Of course, nothing stops you from blogging your book for your own enjoyment—market or no market, too personal a subject or not, appropriate style or not. Readers will show up anyway. You can always tell your friends and family to come read your blogged book. Without a great subject, however, you won't gain many unique visitors, subscribers, or readers, and you likely won't attract an agent or publisher.

So my answer holds true. No, you can't blog a book on just any topic. In fact, if you want to blog a book, you must choose your topic as carefully as if you were planning to write a traditionally published or self-published book.

Just as they say "a rose is a rose is a rose," the same holds true for books, blogged or otherwise. A book is a book is a book.

CAN ANY BLOGGER BECOME A SUCCESSFUL AUTHOR?

If you want to blog a book, I suggest you approach this endeavor like any other book project. This means putting aside your writer's hat and putting on your businessperson's hat before you begin your book project. This allows you to look at the big picture of both your blog and your blogged book just as you would if you were writing an e-book or a printed book. Only when you do this can you decide if your blogged book represents a viable business proposition.

In fact, when you write a book, you create a business. Whether you self-publish that book or a publisher publishes it for you, it becomes a source of income. You also have to promote the book, which means you must develop marketing and promotion plans and implement them. You may go out and speak on the book's topic and earn money doing so; thus you become more than just a writer. You become a professional speaker. You also may decide to offer other services, such as coaching, teleseminars, or home study courses, that relate to your book. All these activities constitute aspects of your business as an author and the particular business center comprised of your book.

For this reason, bloggers or aspiring authors who take a business approach to their blogged books spend time researching their online and physical markets and competition. They also create online promotion plans and develop a strategy for building an author's platform on the Internet and off. And they do this prior to publishing their first post. To decide whether or not their idea is worthy of a blogged book, they ask themselves many questions, including:

- Is my topic unique?
- Does what I have to say add value to my readers?
- Is there a market for this blog or blogged book?
- Who are my readers?
- How is my blog or blogged book different from the competition?
- How will I position myself in the cybermarket or brick-and-mortar market?
- What will I include in my blogged book?
- How will I organize the blogged book (and, thereby, my blog)?

In chapters three and four, we'll delve deeper into the business side of blogging your book. In the meantime, ask yourself this question: Are you willing to approach your blogged book like a businessperson or only like a writer or blogger?

If you answered, "Like a writer," maybe you should consider your blog as your daily writing practice instead of as a book project.

If you said, "Like a blogger," maybe you should simply pick a topic about which you feel passionate and write a few times a week for the joy of covering your topic; don't worry about whether or not your posts come together in any type of logical sequence. Maybe at some point in the future you'll decide to book your blog.

If you said, "As a businessperson," you've joined the ranks of the most successful bloggers and nonfiction writers. Congratulations. In this day and age successful bloggers and nonfiction writers must also be savvy businesspeople.

Next I'll discuss the advantages of blogging a book. After all, if you are going to consider blogging a book rather than writing a book in a more traditional and private manner, you will want to fully understand the reasons you should do so.

CHAPTER 2:

WHY BLOG A BOOK?

Before I discuss the real "business" of blogging a book—or deciding if you actually have a book to blog, let's take a closer look at the advantages of blogging a book rather than simply writing a book the old-fashioned way. In the introduction, I told you why I blogged a book. Why should you do the same?

If you write a book the traditional way, you have two options: You can self-publish it in some form (this may mean blogging it, producing a print-on-demand (POD) version, printing self-published copies in volume to distribute and sell, or producing an e-book). Or you can get it published traditionally, which involves writing a book proposal and finding an agent to approach a midsized or large publishing house for you or approaching a small publishing house on your own. I see ten major reasons to blog a book.

REASON #1: A BLOG ALLOWS YOU TO PUBLISH AS YOU WRITE

Each time you write a blog post and hit the "publish" button, you have, indeed, published your work. You have sent it out to the World Wide Web for anyone and everyone to read. You have become a publisher. You have self-published your copy. You have become an author as well as a blogger.

Therefore, blogging a book gives you the opportunity to actually publish your book as you write it rather than waiting until you complete your manuscript. You stop waiting for someone else to say you are a good enough writer to have your work published or to say your work is good enough for them to publish for you, and you simply publish it yourself in cyberspace.

For many aspiring authors, a blog represents their first byline. If you've never had your writing published before, you'll find a blog a thrilling first publishing experience—one in which you get to become the editor and publisher, and all the cyberworld becomes your possible audience. You get to be in control of what you publish and when you publish it. Wow.

If you have tried for years to find a publisher for your work, you will discover great joy in the fact that when you "submit" (or publish) your blog posts, no rejection letter comes back in return. Instead of watching the mailbox—snail mail or e-mail—you can keep an eye on your blog statistics to see how many readers show up. Yes, readers! You also can watch for comments from your loyal fans. Yes, fans! These activities are lots more fun than opening rejection letters from editors and publishers.

Blogging a book does not mean you have to give up on traditional or self-publishing routes. In fact, you can send literary agents, acquisitions editors, and publishers to your blog to read your writing. You can submit book query letters and proposals as you blog your book. You can produce an e-book or a printed version when you finish blogging your book.

Some writers may not want to "give away" their whole book online. Maybe you worry that a publisher won't want to offer you a contract if you have no new information to offer in a printed version. Or maybe you think your blog readers won't purchase a printed version of your blog if they've already read every post in your blog. Possibly you hear that the continued availability of the information on your blog will deter people from actually purchasing a printed book with the same content.

If you feel this way, you can pick and choose how much of your book to blog. Keep some of your information for a self-published or traditionally published version. That's fine. In fact, it's actually a good idea. I held back two chapters and the conclusion of this book and added more than 32,000 words to the printed version you hold in your hands, more than doubling the book's original page count.

http://howtoblogabook.com

In the meantime, you'll be able to call yourself a published writer and a publisher. You also can call yourself a blogger. And your work will be available for the whole world to read.

Isn't that what all writers really want anyway—for their writing to be available for readers to read?

REASON #2: A BLOGGED BOOK GIVES YOU EXPOSURE AND BUILDS PLATFORM

Many writers enjoy spending time alone in their "lonely garret" with only the company of a hot cup of coffee or tea, a computer (or a pad of paper and a pencil), and a pet of some sort curled up at their feet. In fact, that's what most writers like best.

To become a published author, however, you must come out of the garret and socialize. You must talk with people and engage them in your work. You must get involved and interact with others. If you don't do this, you won't develop an audience for your work. You won't build a base of readers—an author platform—for yourself and for your books.

If *platform* represents new terminology to you, it's time to become familiar with this word … very familiar, very fast.

A strong and sturdy author's platform can consist of a combination of many elements, such as:

- expert status
- numerous appearances on radio and Internet talk shows and television talk and news shows
- frequent guest posts on other people's blogs
- a well-known presence in online forums and social networks
- large numbers of followers on social networking sites
- popular videos, podcasts, or blogs
- frequent interviews on other people's podcasts, videos, or blogs
- your own Internet, radio, or television show
- many published articles or books in print and Internet publications

- an extremely large mailing list
- frequent talks and presentations given to small, medium, and large groups

You don't need all of these platform elements to actually have an author's platform. One of these elements, if large enough, can comprise a platform. The more elements you use to build your platform, though, the stronger and larger it becomes.

Most of the items on this list have little to do with writing. That's what makes blogging such a great platform-building option; it involves writing and lots of it.

Traditionally the best way to build a platform involved going out and speaking to audiences, but today you can speak to your audience online via a blog. In fact, you can speak to a lot more people every day through a popular blog than you ever could via public speaking. (If you want, you can even speak using videos and recordings uploaded easily to your blog as well.)

Imagine one thousand or more people reading your blog every day (a pretty awesome thought). That adds up to a lot of readers per month … enough to impress an agent or a publisher. If even two percent of those readers purchased a book you authored, that would amount to twenty books per day. That's 140 books per week, or over 7,000 books in one year. A publisher would be happy with those sales numbers. According to Nielsen BookScan, a data provider for the book-publishing industry that compiles point-of-sale data for book sales, the average U.S. book now sells less than 250 copies per year and less than 3,000 copies over its lifetime. That's a pretty unimpressive number.

The other platform elements listed above have their place and remain important if you want to become a traditionally published author or sell a lot of self-published books. Remember, however, I said one platform element, if large enough, could produce a sound author's platform? In fact, a successful blog can do just that. If you write a great blog and manage to draw enough readers, this alone can prove impressive enough as a platform element in a book proposal to land you a literary agent or a publisher—with or without other elements.

Let me explain why. New technology, including that which makes blogging a book so easy, hasn't necessarily helped the publishing industry. In turn, this has made it harder for aspiring authors to get their feet in the door at traditional publishing houses. Publishers have become more and more reticent to take a chance on an unknown quantity—a first-time author with no track record of book sales.

It's no wonder, therefore, that according to Bowker, the global leader in bibliographic information management solutions, a staggering 132 percent increase in print-on-demand (POD) books were published in 2009 primarily by independent (self-published) authors; new POD technology made this possible. In July 2010, Amazon reported that e-books were outselling hardcover books—180 e-books for every 100 hardcover books. New technology—e-book readers—made this possible.

These facts represent great news for POD and e-book publishers and authors, but bad news for traditional publishers. According to the statistics on U.S. traditional book publishing released by Bowker in May 2009, U.S. title output dropped from 2007 to 2009, and it has continued its downturn. The number of people buying these traditionally published books declined as well. However, the number of people reading online and reading e-books continued to increase. As their business continues to decline, publishing companies take fewer risks on new authors, put less money into promoting new books, and become more cautious about the books they choose to purchase.

For these reasons, if you blog a book and develop a large blog readership, you become more attractive to a traditional publisher than a writer who has written a manuscript and has no audience or platform as yet. You will have developed a track record—maybe not of book sales but of blog-book readers. Of course, both of you could choose to independently publish your books. If you did, which one of you will likely realize more success? The writer with the blogged book, of course. The prebuilt platform will ensure you have sales upon book release.

REASON #3: A BLOGGED BOOK GIVES YOU EXPERT STATUS

According to Technorati.com, in 2010 56 percent of all bloggers said their blogs helped them or their companies establish positions as thought leaders within their industries. Additionally, 58 percent said they were better known in their industries because of their blogs.

No matter a person's actual credentials, a published book always helps establish expert status. Expert status constitutes one spoke in an author's platform. Publishers and readers purchase nonfiction books from authors they perceive as experts in their fields.

If blogging can help a person—any person—build expert status, imagine what blogging a book can do. It not only can help propel you into the ranks of "thought leader," but also into the ranks of published author.

Of course, you must know your topic. You must have great and well-researched information to offer your blog readers. If you don't, no one will read your blogged book (or blog) or perceive you as anything but a fraud. If you offer superb information in the form of a blogged book, however, little by little—post by post—you will achieve expert status.

That expert status will help you get noticed online and off by readers, agents, and publishers.

REASON #4: A BLOGGED BOOK GETS YOUR WRITING READ—AND READ QUICKLY

Why do writers write? Some might answer, "Because they must." I believe writers write because they want someone to read what they've written.

They write because they want to touch someone with their words. They write because they want to reach out through their work and make others cry, laugh, learn something, be transformed, feel inspired, or in some way relate to their own experiences. They write to take readers on a journey, transport them into another world, or show them a slice of life. They write to help people and to share what they know.

With a traditionally published book, authors might wait a year and a half or two years (or longer) after receiving a book contract for their books to be published. Then they must wait for readers to actually find their books and purchase them. Their books also may appear only in online bookstores, like Amazon.com; getting them onto brick-and-mortar bookstore shelves may or may not happen. Unless authors promote their books well (publishers don't do much promoting these days), readership can remain low. Remember what I told you earlier? Book-Scan reports the average U.S. book sells less than 250 copies per year and less than 3,000 copies over its lifetime.

If you independently publish your book you will not have to wait a year or two while it goes through production. Once you have a completed manuscript and a book design and a cover, your book can arrive in your hands and in online bookstores in four to six weeks, sometimes less. Without good promotional efforts, though, you'll still lack readers, which means buyers.

Great promotional efforts (and a great book worth reading) draw readers. This means you will, indeed, have your writing read. It's possible to sell well over 250 copies per year and to reach larger numbers than average over the book's lifetime.

A blogged book works differently from a printed book. The more you write and the more you promote that writing (on the Internet and elsewhere), the more readers you attract. Just as with a printed book, if you have a good idea that adds value to readers' lives or touches them emotionally, people will want to read your blogged book. Therefore, they will "purchase" it; they will subscribe to your blog or come by each day to read what you have posted. They will keep reading.

You do not have to wait to publish, or release, your blogged book. When you decide you are ready to begin publishing your posts, you can hit the "publish" button and release that first post—a bit like your first installment—into cyberspace. Voilà! Your book can now attract readers. Of course, the whole book does not become available immediately; you release it post by post, day by day, as you write your manuscript. In this manner, your book gets read much more quickly than it might with a traditionally published or self-published book. (More on how to publish your posts in chapter six.)

When you begin publishing posts, you might have no readers. This is not unlike having no buyers. Then you'll have one … two … three. (You can track this with a blog's statistics program.) Before you know it, you'll have twenty readers a day. Then, you'll have fifty readers a day. That equals 350 readers in one week. That's more readers in one week than the average traditionally published author has in a year.

Why blog a book? Because your writing will get read—and it will get read more quickly than it would using other publishing methods.

REASON #5: A BLOGGED BOOK ALLOWS YOU TO TEST-MARKET YOUR BOOK

No better way exists to test-market a book than to blog it into existence. Every good businessperson knows the value of test-marketing a product before investing a ton of money into mass production and distribution. Value exists in test-marketing a book as well, and a blogged book represents an extremely effective and cheap way to test-market a book idea.

My former agent once told me to write and then self-publish one of my book ideas as a test-marketing method. If it sold well, he said he'd take it on. You see, if I had good sales figures for the book, if I could prove the book would sell and had a market, then my agent felt assured he could pitch it successfully to a major publishing house and land a publishing contract for me. Publishers want to know books have markets and readers who are waiting and ready to purchase a book. Publishers want a sure bet, not a long shot, especially with a first-time author.

However, while getting traditionally published offers a writer superb clout, by the time you've gone to the time, trouble, and expense of self-publishing to test-market your book, you might not care about a traditional publishing deal any longer. You might find this especially true if you've managed to achieve success with your self-published book.

What if your self-publishing test-market venture fails and you sell just twenty copies, though? Then you are out the time, effort, and money you put into your business experiment. And your dream of traditional publishing as well.

Consider instead blogging your book as a test-marketing exercise. Simply put bits of your book out into cyberspace each day or several times a week for free (or almost for free). If readers are interested, and you have something worth reading, they will appear out of nowhere!

If they don't come, well, then your test-marketing has succeeded in demonstrating that your idea does not have merit, needs to be tweaked, needs more promoting, or should be aimed at a different market. Or maybe your "product" should be thrown into the circular file.

http://howtoblogabook.com

A blog is free or cheap, and easy to destroy. If this blogged book doesn't pan out the way you hoped, just delete it. You can start another blog tomorrow just as easily and cheaply. Go back to the drawing board and try blogging a book on another topic.

Remember, though, you do have to give the blog some time and put in the promotional and marketing effort to get it out there. Know that—and do that—before you simply decide after a week or two that your test-marketing effort has proven your idea a failure. It may not be a failure. Your promotional efforts might have failed or been insufficient.

Blogs take a while to catch on—even with good promotion. Give your blog at least six months to a year (with really great promotion) before you decide to hit the delete button. Bill Belew, a professional blogger (that means he makes money blogging), claims new bloggers must post three times a day at a minimum until they reach one thousand posts if they want to accrue "real" traffic to their blogs. The posts need only be about 250 words long. At that point, their traffic—readership—skyrockets. (See his book, *How Wilby Got 20 Million People To Read His Blog and How You Can Too.*) Not only that, imagine how many words you would have written. That's 250,000 words or five books in about ten months!

Technorati ranks blogs by something called "Authority," which involves standing and influence in the blogoshere. (You can find more on this topic in chapter seven.) According to the 2011 Technorati State of the Blogosphere report, the Technorati top 100 bloggers by Authority posts to their blogs more than 600 times per month, which equates to more than twenty times per day. The Technorati top 500 bloggers by Authority posts to their blogs more than 350 times per month, which equates to more than ten times per day, and the Technorati top 5,000 bloggers by Authority posts to their blogs more than 100 times per month, which equates to more than four times per day. That should give you an idea of what it takes to get your blog noticed in the blogosphere.

Gina Trapani posted to her blog, http://lifehacker.com, twelve times a day every weekday for nine months. This got her an e-mail from an agent and a book deal for what became *Lifehacker: 88 Tech Tricks to Turbo Charge Your Day* (Wiley 2006).

Not all people want to subscribe to a blog that sends them three or twelve posts a day, though. You need to know your readers, determine how fast you want to blog your book, and decide to what type of writing and posting schedule you can commit. I'm simply making the point that you do need to blog often and for a fairly long period of time—and promote that blog so people know it exists—before you actually begin to see a decent number of readers. In fact, it can take more than a year before you know if your blog has an audience. On the other hand, with really great promotion and lots of blog posts, you might know in a month or two if your market responds favorably. Plus, after six to twelve months, your book will be written and you will be ready to self-publish it as an e-book even if you haven't garnered a ton of readers. There's hardly any cost in producing an e-book, and you might make a bit of money in sales, so your work will not be for naught. You also can self-publish a print book if you like.

Just like a potential reader goes to the bookstore or to Amazon.com to purchase a book, they search online for blogs to read. If they find your blogged book among the thousands—no millions—of others and like it, they'll "buy" it, meaning they'll return more than once to read it or they'll subscribe to your RSS (really simple syndication) feed so it shows up in their browser each time you post. Maybe they'll even subscribe to it via e-mail, if you provide that option. They'll also tell their friends about it by sharing the link to your blogged book. (This is a bit like giving someone a copy of a book.)

If a lot of people do this, you'll know you've got a winning book on your hands. If they don't, you'll know you need to go back to your research and development phase. Either way, you'll have successfully completed your test marketing.

REASON #6: A BLOGGED BOOK PROVIDES A DAILY WRITING COMMITMENT

Writers write. That's what we're told. However, often writers don't write.

If you blog a book, you must write regularly. Hopefully, the blog becomes a form of daily writing practice or a daily writing commitment.

Once you begin blogging, to gain readers you must post frequently. The more often you post, the more quickly you'll gain readers. Remember what the professional blogger said: You need to write three posts a day until you reach one thousand posts. Or you can just post three times a week; that's enough, too. I posted one time a day on weekdays for eleven months on my blog Writenonfictionnow.com. I then cut back to three days a week and now post Monday, Wednesday, and Friday. On Howtoblogabook.com, I wrote three or four times a week for five months, until I had finished the manuscript. Then I tapered off to once a week or so.

The more often you write, the faster your readership will grow. The more content on your blog, the more likely the spiders, bots, crawlers, and such (the automated processes that search engines like Google and Yahoo use to index billions of Web pages) will discover your blog. When they do, your blog will get search engine ranking, which makes it possible for readers to find you. Someone searching for your topic on Google, for instance, will discover your blogged book because your link comes up on a search page—hopefully the first one. Producing lots of keyword-rich content—content with words related to your topic that might be used in an Internet search—provides one of the best search engine optimization (SEO) tools around. (More on this in chapter six.)

Blogging a book, rather than just blogging, means you provide a continuous flow of posts. Most blogs have random, unconnected posts. A blogged book must have posts that follow in a logical sequence, just like the content in any printed book. (However, each post stands alone as well.) In fact, your readers will be waiting for their next installment. This provides even more incentive to you—the blogger—to write on a regular schedule. It also provides incentive for readers to return.

Consider employing deadlines that inspire you to write regularly. In addition to making a commitment to posting every day, every other day, or three to four times per week, you might want to post at a certain time or on certain days. Such commitments help ensure you actually do the work.

I blogged this book by writing three to five posts per week. I did not write them on a schedule. I had no deadline other than my quota of posts per week. I could, however, have required that I posted them on Monday, Wednesday, Friday, and sometimes Saturday, too, at 10 A.M. Then my blog readers would have known when to expect a new post. (I didn't do this because I didn't want the stress of the added deadline. Plus, I had no problem writing the book regularly without that extra incentive.) As I already mentioned, I have another blog where my readers do expect me to publish a post on Monday, Wednesday, and Friday. I try to do so in the morning so the post gets the most exposure during the day in all time zones across the U.S., but sometimes I squeeze it in late in the day or evening. I rarely miss posting on that schedule, though.

With this sort of commitment and daily or regular writing practice, your book surely will get written. When I wrote the post that made up this section of this book, I already had completed 5,000 words by simply writing about 300 words per post over the course of about five weeks. That's not a lot of words per day. In fact, you could write more and post more often. You could post three times a day and write about 1,000 words per day. You'd complete your book fairly quickly and gain readers much faster as well.

REASON #7: A BLOGGED BOOK ALLOWS YOU TO GET FEEDBACK ON YOUR WRITING

The fact that readers have the ability to comment on your book offers you, the blogger, one of the greatest reasons to blog a book. This aspect of blogging a book goes beyond test-marketing and allows readers to give you feedback, ask questions, dialogue with you, and generally tell you how they feel about your product. Plus, you can engage in a conversation with your blog readers almost like you would in a focus group.

Many writers join critique groups so they can have other writers read or listen to them read their work and offer feedback. However, when you, the blogger, receive comments from your blog readers via the comment feature, you hear from the actual people who would purchase your book in a bookstore. This offers you invaluable feedback.

The comment function on a blog also offers you a chance to enter into a dialogue with your readers. When they choose to comment on what you have written, you can reply and ask readers questions or attempt to get them to continue conversing with you about the book, its content, your writing, etc. Since these people represent your true readers, they offer the best feedback possible—even better than members of a critique group.

It's also possible to put surveys on your blog. Then you can ask your readers how they feel about what they are reading, if they are interested in reading about certain topics, or what aspects of the blog they find useful. This type of input from your readers can prove invaluable as well; you can implement the information you receive immediately by going back and rewriting or editing posts, adding posts, or altering your writing strategy on future posts.

In addition, you can add a forum to your blog. This allows readers to form a community. In this manner, you can discover their interests and concerns, which provide you with fodder for your blogged book. It also gives you another way to ask them questions about your book for the purpose of feedback.

REASON #8: A BLOGGED BOOK ENSURES YOU COMPLETE YOUR MANUSCRIPT

Many writers start book projects and don't finish them. This is especially true for nonfiction writers who want to become traditionally published. Unlike fiction writers, who must submit a completed novel along with a brief proposal to an agent or acquisitions editor, nonfiction writers must only submit about twenty-five pages of a completed manuscript as part of their book proposal. If they then wait for a publishing deal, they may never finish their book. Instead, they may go on to work on another book proposal, starting the next book and never finishing that one either (if they fail to hook the interest of a publisher).

As part of a book proposal, a nonfiction writer needs a platform; without a platform the traditional publishing contract may never show up. Since having a presence on the Internet represents one board in a platform, you might as well blog your book while you wait for an agent to pick you up and for an offer to come in from a publisher. Blogging your book will prevent you from stopping your writing activity at page 25.

Believe me, I know the value of this. I have at least five or six book proposals completed. That means I also have about five or six books started and not finished.

You might argue that anyone can start a blog and then stop writing it at any time. You can even delete it. It would disappear from cyberspace as fast as it showed up.

I can't disagree with this argument. Consider, however, your readers. What would they think if you suddenly stopped writing?

Here's my point: Once your blog has even a few regular readers, you are more inclined to keep blogging your book until you've completed the whole manuscript. Your readers and subscribers become your "accountability partners." You know they wait for you to post something. You know they want you to complete the book. They want to "turn the page"; they want to finish reading the book. You can't let them down. You have to act responsibly and keep writing until you've posted the last word of your manuscript.

If you stop in the middle, you disappoint all your readers. You fail publicly. No one likes to do that.

I end up feeling guilty when I don't publish a blog post for a few days. (I have five blogs and two online columns.) I can't imagine how badly I would feel if I just stopped writing a book I was composing in real time in cyberspace if I knew people were reading it.

That's why I argue that no better way exists to ensure you finish your manuscript than to blog your book.

REASON #9: A BLOGGED BOOK SHOWS WHAT YOU'VE GOT ... BUT NOT ALL YOU'VE GOT

A lot of people ask me whether they should include everything in their blogged book. They are afraid to "give it all away." In fact, no need exists to give it all away if you don't want to do so.

It's true that if you blog every last word of your manuscript and publish it in cyberspace:

- a publisher might not want to offer you a contract for a printed book.
- some readers might not want to purchase your self-published book or e-book because you aren't offering new content.

You can get around these issues and still blog your book. If you hold back some of your material, you can:

- attract a publisher with the fact that you still have plenty of new material to of-fer—and your blog readers already love what you've written and published.
- convince your loyal blog-book readers they should buy your self-published book or e-book because it contains more of the great information you pro-vide on your blog.

Actually, agents and acquisitions editors like it if you hold back a bit so they have new material to include in the printed version of your book—should you wind up with an actual publishing contract. Not showing all your posts, so to speak, can offer an advantage in the form of added value for a publisher. They don't want to reduce the value of what's available online, but they do want to add value to what will be available in a printed book.

Should you decide to self-publish your blogged book, you might want to keep the same principle in mind. From this perspective, you could consider your blogged book a skeleton of the complete book. You might provide most, but not all, of the material, and go back later to fill in the gaps. You can use it as a way to write full steam ahead without stopping to worry about the missing pieces, and only going back to handle those when you get ready to do your second and more complete version.

For many writers, this feels much less stressful and overwhelming. There-fore blogging a book becomes an easier and more pleasant way to write a book, or the first draft of a book. It can also prove a faster way to complete your first draft.

As I edited my blogged book, I found I added and changed a fair amount; the word count more than doubled. Plus, as I mentioned. I purposely left two whole chapters out of the blog, with a plan to make them added features in the printed book.

REASON #10: A BLOGGED BOOK LETS YOU AND YOUR BOOK GET DISCOVERED!

Editors and acquisitions editors from publishing houses continue to troll the Internet in search of successful blogs as fodder for new printed books. One of those deals could have your name on it.

If you want your blog to get discovered:

- Pick a topic about which you feel passionate.
- Know you'll have enough material to keep you writing for a long time.
- Be sure other people are interested in your topic.
- Make sure you are adding something new and unique to the overcrowded blogosphere.
- Write great content (content readers want, need, enjoy, or connect with emotionally) often and consistently.
- Promote your blog and your posts well.
- Don't give up.

If this list seems overwhelming to you right now, don't despair. You'll find all the information you need to accomplish these things in the following chapters—with the exception of the determination to keep going, which you must create for yourself. To help with that, I suggest you familiarize yourself with some of the blog-to-book success stories out there. This will keep you inspired. You can find interviews with five of those people in chapter ten, but here's a rundown on just a few of the more well-known blog-to-book deals.

Julie Powell received a book contract for a memoir she wrote based on her blog The Julie/Julia Project. This book was then made into the 2009 hit movie *Julie & Julia*, written and directed by Nora Ephron. Powell blogged about cooking all of the 524 recipes in Julia Child's *Mastering the Art of French Cooking* during a single year. Ephron's screenplay is adapted from *My Life in France*, Child's autobiography written with Alex Prud'homme, and Powell's memoir.

Lizzie Skurnick received a publishing contract for a children's literature/young adult book from HarperCollins for her blog at Jezebel.com, called *Fine Lines*. In this column, Skurnick analyzes classic young adult books, deconstructing them with wisdom, humor, and incredible insight. The book, *Shelf Discovery*, includes work that has appeared on the blog, as well as new work.

In England, Salt Publishing offered Emily Benet, who originally wrote under the name Belle de Jour, a contract for her blog, Shop Girl Blog, about a twenty-eight-year-old call girl's sexual exploits. *Shop Girl Diaries* won a Guardian award, and rumors have it she landed a six-figure deal.

Sex After Sixty was discovered by the e-book publisher 3ones as Mary L. Tabor wrote her memoir live for all of cyberspace to read. It is now available as an e-book and a print book called *(Re)Making Love: A Sex After Sixty Story* (Outer Banks Publishing Group).

Shreve Stockton's *Daily Coyote* blog, which contained photos of and commentary about the coyote pup she raised after its parents were shot, was published by Simon & Schuster and given the same name.

Ben Huh acquired the Fail Blog in January 2008 with his company, Pet Holdings. It contains a collection of photos and videos depicting various kinds of failure. After being contacted by several agents, Huh sold it to William Morrow Paperbacks, who turned the blog into *Fail Nation: A Visual Romp Through the World of Epic Fails.*

Pamela Slim started blogging as an assignment for a class about building platform and online business. Her blog, Escape from Cubicle Nation, shows readers how to bust out free from their three gray walls and start businesses. She received a book deal from *Portfolio Hardcover for Escape from Cubicle Nation: From Corporate Prisoner to Thriving Entrepreneur*, a guidebook containing her best material.

Walker Lamond's blog offered fatherly advice on how to be a good man. He got a deal from St. Martin's for *Rules for My Unborn Son*, which, like the blog by the same name, offers a collection of advice from father to son.

Stuff White People Like, by Christian Lander, reportedly got a $350,000 advance from Random House Trade Paperbacks for this satirical look at stereotypical behavior of white people. The book and the blog share the same name.

Postcards From Yo Momma, a blog by *The Observer's* Doree Shafrir and Jezebel's Jessica Grose, includes entries about stupid e-mails written by mothers. The book version, *Love, Mom: Poignant, Goofy, Brilliant Messages from Home*, was contracted by Hyperion.

Here's my favorite: During the worst year of his life, Canadian Neil Pasricha decided to try to focus on the positive and come up with one thousand simple, free awesome things most people take for granted, posting one each day on his blog, 1,000 Awesome Things. Pasricha won two Webby awards, which are known as the Oscars of the Internet, and a book deal. *The Book of Awesome*, published by Amy Einhorn Books/Putnam contains two hundred of his awesome things.

Other bloggers who have landed deals include:

- Leo Babauta's *Organized Simplicity*
- Brett and Kate McKay's *The Art of Manliness*
- Joe Ponzion's *F Wall Street*
- Laurie Perry's (Crazy Aunt Purl) *Drunk, Divorced & Covered in Cat Hair*
- Grace Bonney's *Design Sponge*

Have I convinced you? Of course these writers drove traffic to their websites. They wrote great content. They blogged often. Some of them even contacted agents. And they were discovered. More bloggers have done the same.

You can do what they did. In fact, you can do better than they did. You can do better than just blog. You can blog a book. And you can be discovered while you do so.

I've given you ten good reasons to blog a book. Now it's time to look at the nitty-gritty process of actually planning and blogging a book.

CHAPTER 3:

HOW TO PREPARE TO BLOG YOUR BOOK

A blogger can simply begin blogging on any topic. If, of course, that blogger wants to attract a lot of readers so an agent or acquisitions editor takes notice and "discovers" him and his blog or blogged book, that blogger needs to do some serious planning prior to publishing the first post. To ensure you build platform and get your blogged book noticed—by readers, agents, and acquisitions editors—prepare to blog your book before you write word one on that blank computer screen or post it on the Internet.

CHOOSE A TOPIC

To begin blogging a book, you must first choose a topic. While this step seems pretty obvious, there's more to it than meets the eye. You can choose any old topic and start writing, or you can choose a topic that attracts readers. I suggest you do the latter.

Of course, you also can—and should—choose a topic that interests you *and* interests a lot of people. Optimally that's what you want to do. In fact, it's best to choose a topic you feel passionate about since you'll be covering it for a long time. You don't want to choose a topic you'll dread blogging about each day. You want the writing to be both fun and interesting and your subject to motivate you to post.

Even better, find a topic about which you feel a sense of purpose—a mission. When you feel compelled to write about a topic because you are fulfilling a purpose, more than likely you also will feel passionate about that topic. When you combine your sense of purpose with your passion, you will become inspired to write about your topic. This will come through in every post, in turn inspiring those who read your blogged book. If your topic also interests others—that is, it has a market—you've chosen a winner.

Knowing something about your topic helps, but you can research your topic as you write if you are not an expert on the subject. Your blogged book will have to contain expert information, though, so be certain the information is available. Many people who write books find it necessary to conduct much research to complete their manuscripts. The same holds true for a blogged book. You can become the expert on your topic if you are willing to put in the time and effort.

If your topic meets four or five of the above criteria, your blogged book will achieve at least some degree of success. Here's a quiz to help you determine if your topic has a chance of becoming a successful blog or blogged book:

1. Does your topic interest you?
2. Does your topic interest a lot of people?
3. Do you feel passionate about your topic?
4. Do you feel you can write about this topic for a long time—several years?
5. Are you an expert on your topic?
6. If you aren't an expert on your topic, can you find information about it easily or access other experts to help you find information?
7. Do you have a sense of mission or purpose about your topic?

If you answered yes to questions 1 through 4 and 6, your topic may, indeed, be a winner. An affirmative answer to questions 5 and 7 increase that likelihood; however, these criteria are not necessary for success, just helpful.

At this point, you might want to check with some of the blog directories or aggregators, like Technorati.com or Blogcatalog.com, or simply perform a search for blogs on Google, specifying your subject to see what other blogs exist on your topic. Then choose a unique angle for your blog. You want your blog to stand out from the crowd of other bloggers writing on your subject. The fact that you are blogging a book on the subject will set you apart to some extent, since most other bloggers will simply be blogging on your topic, but you'll need a bit more of a hook than that. So consider what others are writing about and choose an angle that works for you and that is different from what others have already chosen.

In the next chapter we will discuss in further depth how to analyze the competition in your subject area.

DECIDE WHY YOU WANT TO WRITE THIS BOOK

This may seem like a silly question, but why do you want to blog (or write) a book?

Think about it . . . What do you want to achieve by blogging (or writing) this book? What's your purpose?

- Do you want to help others?
- Do you have knowledge you feel compelled to share?
- Do you feel you can change the world with your story?
- Is the timing just perfect for you to blog (write) this book?
- Have you been waiting for years for science to catch up with your theories and just yesterday someone revealed new evidence to support what you've known all along?
- Do you have the solution to a problem and feel you must share it?
- Does a (blogged) book offer you a way to gain customers for your business?
- Will a (blogged) book prove you are an expert on your subject?

I mentioned earlier that a purpose or mission makes it easier to blog a book because you will be writing about your topic for a long time—probably long past the time when you finish blogging the actual book. It gives you the incentive to keep on writing. Additionally, if your book shares your sense of purpose it gives readers an incentive to keep on reading. That's why your blogged book must fulfill your purpose or mission. This gives it a reason to exist. If your blogged book doesn't have a purpose or mission, no one will show up at your blog to read the posts day after day (the equivalent to turning the pages of a printed book).

The big question you must answer is: What's your mission? In other words, what do you want to accomplish by blogging this book? Do you have some driving reason you must blog this book now? Does doing so fulfill your purpose? What's in it for you? What will you get out of writing this book? Wealth? Fame? Clients? Expert status? Satisfaction? A new business? Fulfillment? And what's in it for your readers? A solution? Much needed help? A journey? An experience?

I must point out that if you are blogging a book for the express purpose of furthering your image, status, or business, your blog and book may not achieve the kind of success you desire. The kind of purpose or mission I'm talking about goes deeper. At the risk of sounding out there, New Agey, and spiritual and possibly turning some of you off, I'm going to stress that you want to consider whether you have a purpose that comes closer to your soul purpose. Maybe this relates to the reason you began doing the work you do. Did you feel called to become a doctor, lawyer, politician, parent, artist, writer, techie, accountant, or whatever you are? Why? What did you hope to accomplish? Who did you hope to help? What were your grand hopes and dreams? Therein lies the reason you are blogging your book. It is your purpose or mission. And therein lies the purpose or mission your book must fulfill as well.

Why must you write this book? Get really clear about the answer. Write it down. Compose a mission statement; i.e., one paragraph that describes why you feel compelled to write or blog this book now.

CREATE A TITLE FOR YOUR BOOK

Your blogged book (or any book) needs a title, and possibly a subtitle, that entices readers into its pages or posts. Sometimes books have creative titles. Not everyone who blogs a book writes nonfiction, but nonfiction does lend itself well to being blogged. Many nonfiction books have tell-it-like-it-is titles that let readers know exactly what they will find within a book's pages. Titles like this make it easier for readers to find your blogged book on the Internet because they come up easily when search terms are put into a search engine. Search terms are the words and phrases people type into the search forms of search engines, like Google, Bing, Internet Explorer, or Yahoo. If you are writing fiction, consider the fact that your title must be something that tells readers what your book is about or that is related to it in some way; if it is a very creative title, readers conducting Internet searches won't find it easily.

To come up with a great title, get clear about your book's subject matter. If you are having trouble coming up with a title, you might still be unclear about your topic or its angle. Skip ahead to the next two sections, "Hone Your Subject" and "How to Write a Pitch for Your Blogged Book," and complete them. Then study how you have described your book. Look for phrases and words that might work in a title.

Often, titles use a play-on-words, alliteration, the actual name of the subject being written about, or a popular phrase. Sometimes titles evoke emotion. The title of a self-help and how-to book should identify or solve a problem, give a reader hope, be easy to remember, or be clear and specific to the topic.

Short titles are more memorable. Numbers work well, too, as in "7 Steps to…" or "10 Ways to…," and "The 8 Places You Should…". The most important thing to remember with blogged books, though, is to use keywords or keyword phrases in your title and subtitle. These are the words or phrases on your website or blog that match search terms. Doing so makes it easier for the people seeking information to find your blogged book on the Internet.

Here are some examples of blog titles and the corresponding book titles that resulted from their blog-to-book deals:

- David McRaney's blog: You Are Not So Smart, a Celebration of Self-Delusion
    - Book title: *You Are Not So Smart: Why You Have Too Many Friends on Facebook, Why Your Memory is Mostly Fiction, and 46 Other Ways You're Deluding Yourself* (Gotham, October 2011)
- Leo Babauta's blog: Zen Habit
    - Book title: *The Power of Less: The Fine Art of Limiting Yourself to the Essential, in Business and in Life* (Hyperion, December 2008)
- Lisa Fain's Blog: Homesick Texan
    - Book Title: *The Homesick Texan Cookbook* (Hyperion, September 2011)

- Matt Gallagher's blog: Kerplunk, One Soldier's Journey from Baghdad to Brooklyn
    - Book title: *Kaboom, Embracing the Suck In a Savage Little War* (<u>Da Capo Press</u>, March 2010)
- Shauna James Ahern's Blog: Gluten Free Girl
    - Book Title: *Gluten-Free Girl and the Chef, A Love Story with 100 Tempting Recipes* (Wiley, September 2010)
- Tucker Max's blog: The Tucker Max Date Application
    - Book title: *I Hope They Serve Beer in Hell* (Citadel, January 2006)
- Zoe McCarthy's blog: My Boyfriend is a Twat
    - Book Title: *My Boyfriend Is a Twat, A Guide to Recognizing, Dealing and Living with an Utter Twat* (Friday Project, August 2007)
- Laurie Perry's blog: Crazy Aunt Purl, The True Life Diary of a Thirty-Something, Displaced Southerner Living in Los Angeles with a Herd Of Felines. Because Nothing Is Sexier Than a Divorced Woman with Three Cats.
    - Book title: *Crazy Aunt Purl's Drunk, Divorced and Covered in Cat Hair, The True-Life Misadventures of a 30-Something Who Learned to Knit After He Split* (HCI, October 2007)

I've mentioned a number of other blogs turned into books in the first two chapters of this book. Of course, my blog, How to Blog a Book: How to Publish Your Manuscript on the Internet One Post at a Time became *How to Blog a Book*.

Notice that many blogs have fairly long taglines that serve as subtitles of sorts. These are often shortened or rewritten into a subtitle for the book. Mine is a good example, as is the one used by *Crazy Aunt Purl* (Laurie Perry).

Now it's your turn. Write a title and subtitle or tagline for your blogged book. Don't worry too much about it being set in stone. As you've seen, they often change when it comes time for a printed version.

HONE YOUR SUBJECT

While you might think you know what you're blogging about, it's always good to hone your subject. You can do that in a variety of ways, such as writing a synopsis or creating an outline of your book. However, when you can distill your idea down to one, or possibly two, short sentences easy to actually speak aloud, you get to the point of really, truly knowing what your book is about. For this reason, I find writing a *pitch* offers the best method for honing your subject.

A pitch, also called an elevator speech—the one you might give to an agent or an acquisitions editor if you happen to meet one in an elevator or at a conference, describes your blogged book in fifty words or less. (I usually tell my coaching clients to describe their books in twenty-five words.) Your blogged book's synopsis or outline might be a page or more in length. Try telling someone about the contents of your synopsis or outline quickly—in one or two minutes or less—off the top of your head. It's difficult to do. However, giving someone your pitch—pitching them—is easy. Why? Because once you've written that pitch you know the subject of your book. You've honed it to a fine point—just twenty to fifty words. It's short and easy to remember. You'll remember it every time you sit down to write a blog post and every time someone asks you what you are blogging a book about. (If you'd like to learn more about pitches in general, you might want to read *Making the Perfect Pitch: How to Catch a Literary Agent's Eye* by Katharine Sands.)

If you do decide you want agent representation, you'll need a pitch. Most aspiring authors pitch an agent or an acquisitions editor at some point.

On the other hand, if you intend to self-publish, you may not plan on pitching your blogged book to agents or editors. Write a pitch anyway so you hone your idea to the max. Once you've written the pitch, your book will naturally flow out of it. You'll find that it becomes much easier to write your manuscript. That's the beauty of having written a pitch—and as good a reason as any for going to the trouble of doing so.

After you've used your pitch to hone your subject, your pitch will come in handy. Anytime you tell someone about your book or your blog, you need a pitch. It's a quick and simple marketing or promotional tool for telling people what your blogged book is about—and convincing them to purchase it. You want to have the ability to tell someone the gist of your book in fifty words or less, including the benefits, unique qualities, and highlights of your "story."

The exercise of getting ready to blog your book involves getting clear about what you are blogging about, why you are blogging a book, and how you are going to move forward both with your writing and blogging. A pitch does this for you. It's the starting point for your writing and for all your promotion and marketing. Once you can tell someone in a short, pithy statement what your blogged book is about, everything falls into place. You know what your book is about, for whom you are writing, what benefit they will derive from your book, and what you must deliver in its pages.

How to Write a Pitch for Your Blogged Book

To write your pitch, start by describing the subject of your blogged book in seventy-five words or less. Then edit this down to fifty words or less. Then see if you can't polish and hone it to about twenty-five words.

To come up with the content for your pitch, start by asking yourself, "What am I writing about?" This reiterates your subject or topic.

To get clear on your book's message, ask yourself, "What am I trying to say to my readers? What do I want readers to remember after they put down my book?" Or answer the question: "Why do I want readers to read my book?"

A pitch should include how your blogged book benefits readers. Try visualizing the back cover of the book. What type of copy might you print there? What would it say? What message would you want to convey about what lies within the pages of your book?

Here are some things to think about and to include:

- Are you giving readers a solution to a problem?
- If you are providing a solution, what is the problem? What is the solution?
- What does your reader want to know?
- What's your goal in writing the book?
- What do you want your readers to achieve from reading your book?
- Why is it important for them to read your book?
- What benefit will they get from reading your book?
- Is your reader in some sort of pain, and can you eliminate that pain?
- Can you make an emotional connection with your readers?
- Who are your readers?

- Is this book timely or time sensitive?

Include the title and subtitle, if you know it, but you don't have to include those in the word count. Sometimes the subtitle actually can serve as part of the pitch.

Writing a pitch shouldn't be too difficult if you know what your book is about and you know why someone should want to read your book. If you know what benefits your book will provide and how it will be unique, you should be able to write something short and pithy that describes your book perfectly.

Why the word limit? People have short attention spans. You have to grab them fast. Plus, if you can't tell someone what your book is about in fifty words or less, then you don't know what you are writing about—and neither will they.

Try your hand at a pitch. Include your book's benefits, its unique qualities, why someone would want to read it, the problem you are going to solve, the value it will add. What makes your book special? At its very core, what is it about? What is its message? What is its purpose? Fit all this information into the most creative twenty-five- to fifty-word sentence or two you can write.

Someone once told me if I couldn't write the subject of my book on the back of a business card, I didn't know what I was writing about. Can you do that? You may not be there yet, but if you go through this exercise, you'll be a lot closer.

MAP OUT THE CONTENT FOR YOUR BOOK

Finally, you need to know what content will go in your book. The best way to make this decision involves creating a "brain dump" of all the subjects you might cover in the book. A brain dump gets all your ideas for your book onto paper so you can organize them. Think of it as uploading into one file all of the data you've been storing in your personal computer that pertains to your subject. You also can conduct a massive brainstorming session on your topic to come up with all the ideas that could possibly become part of your book. Once you've finished your brain dump, you are ready to begin sorting through the material and organizing it into something that looks more like a book outline.

This exercise is most commonly called mind mapping. You can purchase mind mapping software or download free software, like FreeMind. The easiest way to complete the exercise, though, involves purchasing a large poster board and some colored sticky notes. I like the rectangular kind you can use to mark pages in a book as you read but that aren't so shiny you can't write on them. (You can also just use colored pens or markers for this exercise, but then you can't move things around. Some people like to use a white board with erasable markers.)

Put a large sticky note in the middle of the board and write your topic on it. Now start writing related topics on the other sticky notes. If you are a very creative person and not too organized, just write down subjects on the sticky notes and stick them on the board. Don't worry about colors or where you put them. Once you have run out of topics, begin organizing them into related topic areas on the board. Pick up the sticky notes and move them around. The new groupings become chapters. You can use a different colored sticky note at the top of each grouping to indicate its general topic heading. As you group the sticky notes, you might get additional ideas. You can add these into the appropriate group or chapter.

You can color code as you go (if you are that organized). For example, for this book, I might use orange for all the topics related to getting started blogging a book. I might use yellow for all the reasons you might want to blog a book. I might use blue for all the blogs that have received publishing deals. I might use green for all the subjects related to how to write your blogged book.

Each subject grouping becomes a chapter in your blogged book. Each of the sticky notes in the groupings becomes a topic to cover in the chapter. Each topic may represent one post or several, depending upon the depth it deserves or the amount of information you have on that topic. Remember, a blog post tends to be between 250 and 500 words in length.

In chapter six, we will discuss how to write your posts and what to do with this rough book structure. For now, rest assured you have just created the basic content and tentative table of contents of your blogged book. Now you not only know what you are writing about, you also know how you will cover that topic from start to finish, from post to post. I suggest you actually get out a piece of paper or sit down at your computer and type out your table of contents. You also can make a list of all the different blog posts you will cover in each chapter.

If you had difficulty honing your topic by writing a pitch, I suggest you try again after mind mapping your book. You can start over on a new pitch or revise the one you have already written. Getting a clear picture of your blogged book's content goes a long way toward helping you know what your book is about and honing your subject. You can then come back to your mind map and search for gaps, redundancies, or other content issues.

Research vs. Expert Source

While you don't need to be the expert on your subject to blog a book, by blogging about a subject and offering great information you become the expert. I'm a trained magazine journalist, and when I was in journalism school my professors taught me that a good journalist can write about anything by becoming the expert on the subject. A good blogger or book author can accomplish the same by becoming a good journalist and doing superb research.

However, that great information has to come from somewhere. At this point in the blog-a-book process, you must figure out what you need to know—if anything—to write your book. Look at the content you plan to generate and ask yourself what research you need to do, what books you need to read, what experts you need to contact, etc. Do whatever it takes to have all your resources ready at your fingertips before you begin writing so you don't have to stop writing to find necessary information. At the very least, know how and where to find these resources.

You may be able to fill in some gaps later, such as when you write your second draft for a publisher or edit your second draft for your self-published print or e-book version. In many cases, you will need the information immediately to actually write your first draft. You also may want to contact other experts for assistance.

It's also possible that you are the expert source. In this case, you may not require any other resources to get started.

Take time to evaluate whether you are the right person to take on this book project. Do you have the knowledge or do you have the resources and access to experts who can help you compile the information necessary to write this book?

Do you or will you be able to understand the information and disseminate it in an understandable manner for your readers? Can you carry out the project from start to finish given what you have just mapped out?

If you answered yes to these questions, with the steps in this chapter under your belt, you are ready to move on to a less creative endeavor: developing the business plan for your book.

http://howtoblogabook.com

CHAPTER 4:

DEVELOPING YOUR BLOGGED BOOK'S BUSINESS PLAN

Now you have to get serious. Really serious.

Anyone who wants to write a book—blogged or otherwise—needs to go through what I call "the book proposal process." This entails compiling the information necessary for a book proposal. You don't have to write the proposal, but you do need to go through the steps required to gather the figures, data, details, and particulars required for each part of a proposal, and analyze this information to some extent.

As I write this, I can imagine some of you saying, "I don't need to write a book proposal." I know; you plan on simply having your blogged book discovered, and that's a good plan. Even if an agent or acquisitions editor finds you and your blogged book in cyberspace and offers you a traditional publishing contract, though, you will be asked to submit a book proposal. While an agent or acquisitions editor from a publishing house can read your blogged book online and decide if they like your subject matter and your writing, they still will want to know more about you and your plans for your blogged book. Therefore, you want to be ready to write a proposal (or have one already written), should you ever need one.

More important, it behooves anyone who wants to write a book, no matter how they plan on publishing it, to go through the proposal process. By doing so, you create a business plan for your book. You need to do that. Every book needs a business plan of its own. Every aspiring or published author needs to function as a businessperson in addition to a writer if he wants to succeed in the publishing world. So ask yourself if you really want to succeed with your blogged book. If you do, go through the proposal process.

The book proposal has served as the industry standard when it comes to creating a business plan for a book. That's why every traditional publisher requires one—and in large part adopts that proposal as its business plan once it signs a contract with a writer. Publishers also look at it as your business plan—and commitment to them as their business partner—for your book. If you create the same document for your blogged book, you also make a commitment to yourself to follow through on the steps necessary for publishing success.

Don't make the mistake of viewing your blogged book as "just a blog." If you plan to blog a book, look at your blog as a manuscript in the making. Indeed that's exactly what you are creating—a manuscript. Approach this endeavor just as you would any other new book project. Every book project should be evaluated through the lens of a book proposal, just like the acquisitions editor, publisher, and sales and marketing teams at a publishing house would (and will) do before deciding to purchase and publish any new book idea. Every aspect—from content through promotion—should be planned out. As a blogger, you serve as the publisher of your book. Be a good businessperson and require a business plan for your book. Go through the proposal process before you publish the first post.

FOUR REASONS TO LOOK AT YOUR BLOGGED BOOK IDEA THROUGH THE LENS OF A BOOK PROPOSAL

If I haven't yet convinced you, let me give you four good and specific reasons to go through the book proposal process. First, one day you may want to sell this book to a publisher, and you'll need a proposal to do so. I don't know of any traditional publisher that will take on a book without first seeing a completed book proposal.

Second, a book proposal allows you to get a big-picture view of your book. As you compile the information necessary for your proposal, you'll be looking at your book through the lens of an acquisitions editor—critically. This means you'll be evaluating its marketability and value-added potential both in cyberspace and on the bookshelf. You'll have to consider what makes your book unique in the market and how it will fare against the existing competition.

Third, since a book proposal includes a section on promotion, a proposal offers you a chance to think about all the different ways in which you can promote your book, not just as a blogged book but eventually as a printed book as well. In today's world of publishing, promotion is everything. A blogged book constitutes a great first step to developing a readership for your book, but you'll need to do more than just blog your book. You'll need to let people know your blog exists, and that takes promotion.

Fourth, a book proposal requires you to come up with an overview, a list of chapters (or table of contents) and a short synopsis of each chapter. These three things provide you with a starting place for your blogged book (and for your book manuscript). Once you've completed these sections of your proposal, you're almost ready to begin writing your blogged book. You have a writing guide to follow as you blog your book into existence. With these as references, you'll know exactly where your blogged book is going and what promises to keep to your readers along the way.

To begin blogging your book, you don't need a formal and complete proposal. You only need to go through the proposal *process.* Just compile the information necessary for a proposal. Do the required analysis. Hone your topic, decide on your content, and create a promotion plan. After you've done these things, you'll have an extremely clear idea about what your blogged book will include, who will read it, how to make it stand out in the marketplace, and in what ways you will promote it. You'll also know if ways exist to build a business around your book with ancillary products or services. Perhaps even more important, you'll know who your readers are and what your competition looks like, if any exists. This information tells you if you should be blogging on this subject or not.

Completing the proposal process also will tell you who else out there blogs or publishes on your topic. These people might make great joint-venture partners or people with whom to create reciprocal links, make agreements for guest blog posts, or contact for help promoting your book.

THE PARTS OF A PROPOSAL

Even though you won't actually be writing a book proposal—although I encourage you to do so and be ready when an agent or acquisitions editor calls, it's important to know something about a book proposal if you plan to go through the book proposal process. You can find many books on how to write a book proposal. Lots of information exists on the Internet as well. The following list, which is divided into two sections, Introduction and Outline, includes the fourteen vital sections of a book proposal. Sometimes these sections are included in a different order; some books don't include them all. Authors and agents sometimes choose to include additional sections or even attachments. In my experience, most agents and publishers are happy with these.

- Introduction
  - Overview
  - Markets
  - Subsidiary Rights
  - Spin-Offs
  - Promotion
  - Competing Titles
  - Complementary Titles
  - Resources Needed to Complete the Book
  - About the Author
  - Mission Statement
  - Author's Platform
- Outline
  - List of Chapters
  - Chapter Summaries
  - Sample Chapters

Since we are talking about blogging a book, if you don't plan on ever looking for a traditional publisher for your book, and you don't want to go through the whole proposal process or create a complete business plan, you can do just the minimum. This means only planning out your manuscript and focusing on marketability. In this case, you'll want to complete the following sections of a proposal prior to beginning to blog your book.

- Introduction
  - Overview
  - Markets
  - Promotion
  - Competing Titles
  - Complementary Titles
- Outline
  - List of Chapters
  - Chapter Summaries

Completing this abbreviated proposal process will provide you with a good "big picture" of your book. The Introduction points out who will read it, the markets to target with your promotion, what competition your blogged book faces, and what bloggers or authors to target for joint venture projects. You also will have created a promotion plan to help you drive traffic to your blogged book and create platform. The outline gives you your structure: chapters and their content (blog posts). These sections also give you a good overview of how to angle your blogged book so it holds a unique spot in both the online and physical bookstores.

That said, I highly recommend completing all the proposal sections. Better to be ready for the possibility of a traditional book deal if one arises. Plus, you will want to have a well-written bio on your blog site, and your mission statement will focus your work. If you complete the entire proposal process, you will have all the material you need, and you will have evaluated your blogged (and printed) book for success. You will be ready for any opportunity, and you will have set yourself up for the highest likelihood of attracting both readers and publishers.

The Overview

The first section of a book proposal, the overview, includes a lot of information in extremely condensed form because it provides a concise description of your book. If you actually write a proposal and submit it to an agent, this section has a hook (similar to a lead paragraph to an article); a pitch; details about the number of pages, illustrations, etc., you expect to include in the printed book; and information on your book's unique features and benefits, as well as information on the back matter (glossary, appendix, resources).

Writing the overview for your blogged book helps you consider the full scope of your book's concept and its features and benefits. You see your book in totality. Also, just as the first chapter to a book entices a reader to continue reading, the overview of a book proposal entices an agent or acquisitions editor to read the rest of the document and to consider publishing the book.

Once written, your overview serves a variety of marketing purposes. You could use all or part of it in an "About" page on your blog, in promotional material featured in other places or documents (on your website or in material sent to prospective reviewers or people you would like to offer cover blurbs or testimonials), or even as your first blog post in which you describe what your blogged book is about. The first few paragraphs of the overview might become the first paragraphs of the first chapter of your printed book, as a revised version did for this book.

In the last chapter, you did some of the work necessary to write your blogged book overview. You came up with a title and honed your subject into a pitch. You also mapped out your content. Therefore, you now have a clear idea of how you will focus your blogged book, what types of topics you might include, and how you might make it unique. This is great fodder for your overview. You will discover more about these things, and possibly change the focus and angle later when you look at the markets and competition sections of a proposal. For now, the information you have gathered will suffice.

Typically an overview begins with a few sentences or a paragraph or two that grab the reader. As mentioned, this isn't much different from an article; the beginning of the overview could be considered your "lead." Write something compelling.

This could even be the first paragraph or two of your blogged book. For example, here are the first two paragraphs—the lead—to my *How to Blog a Book* proposal:

> For the last five years acquisitions editors have scanned the Internet to find new writers with great ideas that can be turned into books. Based on research done by Publishers Marketplace, experts estimate more than sixty blogs landed book deals in 2009. The database includes only announced deals; the total number was much higher.
>
> Some of the writers who landed contracts simply blogged their way to a deal; some of them blogged actual books. In both cases, they turned out copy that attracted readers' and publishers' attention, and they did it one post at a time on the Internet.

You'll find a semblance of these two paragraphs at the beginning of chapter one of this book. When I revised the manuscript, they changed a bit, and then my developmental editor and line editor asked for more changes. In both forms they provide the necessary hook to get someone—readers or an agent or acquisitions editor—interested in reading further.

Next, insert your pitch—twenty-five to fifty words that describe your book (see chapter three)—followed by a statement that includes how many pages your book will have and how much back matter it will include. If you need a sentence to transition into your pitch, that's fine. Here's the paragraph that followed the copy above in my proposal:

> How can other writers accomplish this feat? The host of aspiring authors hoping their online writing efforts will get them discovered can find the answer to this question in *How to Blog a Book, A Step-by-Step Guide to Writing and Publishing Manuscripts on the Internet One Post at a Time. How to Blog a Book* will be the first book to explain the basics of how to write and publish a successful nonfiction book—one that gets noticed by readers and publishers—in cyberspace. The finished manuscript will contain

approximately 33,500 words, or 134 pages, and will have one page of back matter consisting of a bibliography.

Since your blogged book's form is a body of posts rather than pages, think of your manuscript pages as posts. How many posts will you write? Each post will be 250 to 500 words in length. A short book has about 25,000 words, which translates into about one hundred published book pages; most publishers want at least 45,000 words (I was asked to add 10,000 words and an index to this book), which gets the printed book closer to two hundred published pages. If you assume the average post will be 350 words in length, you will have to write about 72 to 129 blog posts. Your back matter might be some extra blog pages with resources or appendices.

If you want to know how many pages your finished manuscript will have, convert the posts to manuscript pages by doing the math. Come up with an average number of words you will write per post, and multiply this by the number of posts; then divide this by 250 words per manuscript page. This will give you the number of manuscript pages you will have when you are done.

Now write a page and a half or so that describes the benefits of your book. To do so, answer these questions: What will my readers gain by reading my blogged book? Once they finish reading the book, what will they have learned? Why should they read my blog or book? You can even list these as bulleted points. For example, "My readers will:

- Gain an understanding of…
- Learn how to….
- Find out how to….
- Discover the answer to…
- Get tips for…
- Change their…
- Experience…
- Be given the solution to…

The answers to these questions will provide the value-added aspect of your book and the last information necessary for the overview.

Also, if your blogged book will have any special features, such as little boxes in each post with tips, a special post once a month offering a meditation, a workbook element (questions to answer), or funny cartoons, mention them. Include information on how these features make your blogged book unique and add benefit to readers.

When completed, the overview should read like a pithy marketing-oriented book synopsis condensed to about two pages. Consider this your promise to your readers and your enticement to potential book buyers and blog readers.

As you later blog your book, refer to the overview to make sure you deliver on your promises and keep closely to your vision of the book. In this way, the overview becomes a writing guide—another reason to write one. Combine the overview with your table of contents and chapter-by-chapter synopsis (which I discuss shortly) as you write, and you have a strong guide—better than any outline—to keep you on track as you blog your book.

Markets—Do You Know Who Will Read Your Blogged Book?

With the first step in the proposal process completed, it's time to move on to the next section included under the Introduction heading: Markets. Make sure you are wearing your businessperson's hat. No writer's hats allowed.

It's time to meet your readers and to discover how many readers your blog potentially could gain. In general, this represents an exercise in researching whether your blog or blogged book, or your digital or printed book, has a market. Is there anyone out there who will read it? Does anyone out there need your book?

Even though you are blogging a book, you need to know this information for two reasons: First, since you will be the one primarily responsible for promoting your blog, you'll want to discover where to place your promotional efforts. In other words, you want to promote to the right readers or in the right markets. Thus you must take time to identify those readers. Second, and more important, you must find out if you even have potential readers. If no market exists for your blog, you'll be lucky to garner even a few readers for your blogged book. (If this is the case, forget about your blogged book getting discovered and made into a traditionally published book.)

If a market exists for your blogged book, you have a reason to write and publish your work on the Internet (or in physical form). To find out, answer the question, "Is there anybody out there who will read (buy) my book, and if yes, who would that be?" Since you are blogging a book, you want to ask, "Is there anyone out there in cyberspace who will subscribe to my blog or come back every few days to see if I've published a new post—a new installment to my book?" In blogging or website terms, you want to know if you have a large enough market to attract a large number of unique visitors that view many pages when they read your blogged book. However, if you also want to publish a printed book one day, you should be concerned about the market for a printed book on your topic as well.

To discover if your book has a market, start with this step: Describe the audience for your blogged book. Who is your average blog reader? Who would be interested in your topic? Who will subscribe to your blog? Include demographic information if you can. Do your research!

Good places to do this type of research include:

- Clubs or organizations related to your subject. Attend some meetings and see what types of people are members.
- Online forums related to your topic. Join these forums and participate in the discussion; start asking questions to see what types of people are members and where else they hang out online. Then check out these places as well and try to gain some information on the people there.
- Online groups related to your topic, such as those on Facebook or LinkedIn. Again, participate in the groups. Get to know the participants and members.
- Bookstores. Check out what types of people are buying books on your topic.
- Google, Yahoo, Bing, and other search engines. Start poking around. Behave like a good journalist and see what you can discover about the types of people who get involved in all things related to your topic.
- Facebook and Twitter. Ask questions of your followers. They'll enjoy responding.

Now describe large groups of people—actual markets—that will subscribe to your blog. For instance, if your blogged book will appeal to women, this market is huge and would be described this way:

> "According to the 2010 U.S. census, there are 156,842,733 women in the United States."

If your blogged book targets chiropractors, for instance, you might describe your market in this fashion:

> "Based on data from ChiroWeb.com and Manta.com, somewhere between 58,000 and 79,600 chiropractors worked in the U.S. in 2011."

If your blogged book will be directed at the international Muslim market—an enormous one—you might write:

> "Muslims will comprise more than one quarter of the Earth's population by the year 2030, according to a study released in January 2011 by the Pew Forum on Religion and Public Life."

Again, do your research! Do some Google research and find statistics and information on the size of these groups. Check:

- Wikipedia.com
- The U.S. Census Bureau
- Organizations that monitor or report on professionals in your subject area or the profession itself
- Organizations that regulate an industry related to your topic
- Major newspapers and publications, such as *The New York Times*
- Market research companies

Don't be lazy. Answer the question, "Who is the market for my blog?" Wrong answer: People like me. People who like cats. Right answer: Thirty-three percent of U.S. homeowners. Go online and use your favorite search engine and ask the right questions; you will get answers. Ask, for instance, "How many people in the United States own cats?" When I put this query into the Google search engine, I easily discovered that the Humane Society of the United States reported 33 percent of U.S. households own at least one cat as of August 2011.

Once you've done your research, you will know if your blogged book has a market or not. If you have large numbers of people who potentially could be interested in your blog, great! Your blog gets the green light.

Subsidiary Rights and Spin-Offs

If you are writing a complete proposal, the next section to tackle is subsidiary rights. When you sell your book to a publishing house, the publisher acquires primary book rights. As Michael Larsen explains in *How to Write a Book Proposal*, primary rights include publishing the book hardcover, trade paperback, and/or a mass-market paperback; book club rights; selling permission to excerpt part of another work; second-serial rights to excerpt the book or condense it or serialize the whole book in a periodical after publication; reproducing the text in other forms and media; reproducing the text in large-type or a royalty-free Braille edition; selling school editions; photocopying rights to all or part of the book for internal use by a school or business; selling the book through direct-response marketing channels; selling the book as a premium to businesses or nonprofits as a promotional tool; selling the book in bulk to customers outside the book industry; and granting the right to use part of the text to promote the book.

Subsidiary rights include things like television and feature film rights, foreign rights, first- and second-serial rights to excerpt the book before publication, translation rights, rights to produce abridged, unabridged, and dramatized audio and video versions of your book, merchandising rights, and software rights (including the now popular phone apps).

While you are wearing your business hat—which you should still have on—consider whether your book has potential for subsidiary rights. While this section is not necessary to the blog-a-book process, I've included it here so you'd be aware of it.

The spin-offs section constitutes a more pertinent section of a book proposal, but also one not necessary to consider prior to beginning to blog your book. That said, acquisitions editors and agents like to know that you are more than a one-book author. The spin-off section of a proposal asks you look at your first book idea and consider what other books you might write as follow-ups.

Still wearing your business hat, ask yourself: Could my book be a series? Does my book naturally lead me to write books on similar or related topics? Is there a way for me to entice a publisher into a multibook deal?

If you want to be found by an agent or publisher, or if you plan on approaching one yourself, it might be a good idea to be prepared to answer the question, "What other books do you plan to write after this one?" Your answer could make the difference between getting a contract and being turned down.

Additionally, this is a good time to consider what you will do when you finish your blogged book. How will you capitalize upon that success? Having your next book idea lined up and ready to go means you don't lose your readers' attention. That's key to becoming a successful author long term. This type of planning also can prove essential if you want to build a business of any type around your blogged book.

Promotion

For a blogged book, promotion primarily means asking the following question: "How are you going to let the cyberworld know your blog exists?" In other words, how will you "sell" your blog?

It's time to add your social hat to your business and writing hats. To gain readers, you must promote yourself and your blog via social networking. Otherwise no one will know you've created a blog or begun blogging a book. While promotion can involve many activities, including speaking, advertising, search engine optimization, radio and television appearances, and podcasting, as well as social networking, the overriding thrust revolves around increasing public awareness of your blogged book and you as a blogger. To accomplish this, you must do things that are public. That's why I consider promotion a social activity requiring a social hat. I suppose you could put on your public hat, instead. Call it what you like. Just put it on and get ready to use social networking, because it's one of the best tools for publicizing, or promoting, your blog.

The Promotion section constitutes a huge part of any book proposal and of the proposal process, and you also need to think about promoting your blogged book off-line. Why? One day it will become a printed book. You need a plan now to gain readers for it in all forms: as a blogged book, a printed book, and an e-book. Therefore, you must create a promotion plan that encompasses not just the Internet. That said, the Internet is the place to begin your promotional efforts, especially given that you are blogging a book.

Promoting in cyberspace does not mean simply gaining friends on Facebook and followers on Twitter, the most powerful social networking sites. It also means getting out there and participating in forums and commenting on related blogs and online columns. It means joining LinkedIn and getting involved in the groups on that site. It also means getting involved in whatever is new, like Google+, and posting your blog to Reddit.com, as well as forming networks of bloggers who will help you get your blogged book noticed with reciprocal linking and agreements to submit each other's posts to sites like StumbleUpon.com. You'll also need to set up your blog to publish to places like Technorati.com. (I'll talk more about all of this in chapter seven.) And you want to let all your social networks know every time you post a blog. That means including the link along with a short note in a status update.

You also can do more traditional types of promotion. You can:

- send press releases to the media
- publish articles on your book's topic
- set up speaking engagements, workshops, and teleseminars
- send out a newsletter
- use e-zine article-marketing techniques
- make radio and television appearances
- start a television show of your own.

Plus, you can (and should) create an expanded website that hosts your blogged book. That site might offer features that attract visitors and readers, such as articles, surveys, resources, and links to other blogs or your radio show. It can also have a media kit or author's page to help you get media attention and speaking engagements.

When it comes to promotion, you must think and act outside the box. You can create contests, give-aways, and gimmicks to attract attention to your blogged book, your website, and to yourself. You can hire a publicist to help you with this task. All of this falls under the heading of promotion.

Of course, you can also hire a search engine optimization (SEO) specialist. These experts can make your blog or website easier to find, whether blog-book readers or ordinary individuals are doing the searching . They also may be able to advise you about online adverting options.

Most writers don't want to do this work. Their eyes glaze over, and they simply refuse. "I only want to write," they say. If you want your blogged book to be read, which in this case means it must be found on the Internet, you must promote it. Period. If you want it one day to be read in book form, which means purchased, you must promote it out in the "real" world. Period. There is no way around this fact.

You have to promote your blogged book both because you simply want people to read it and also so that an acquisitions editor will find it. You must have readers (and a good many at that) for an acquisitions editor to find your blogged book and feel it deserves to be published. You'll need to have gained large numbers of friends, followers, "tweeple," and connections in your social networks. You'll need a large number of unique visitors who seek out your blog. You'll also want your blog to have a sizeable subscriber and email list as well. All of these figures go into a written proposal as part of your Platform section, but come into play in the Promotion section as well.

Consider speaking publicly on the topic of your blogged book, making radio and television appearances, doing workshops and teleseminars, writing a newsletter, going on a speaking tour, or anything else you can think of to promote your book. Include all of these activities in your promotion plan.

The Promotion section can make or break a formal book proposal. Publishing houses rely on you to come up with a great promotion plan; it becomes *their* promotion plan. A publisher will add to your plan, but primarily relies on you to promote your own book in your own way. Most publishing houses do little these days to help promote new titles, especially those from first-time authors.

If you self-publish your book, your promotion plan becomes your business plan. This is your strategy for selling books. When you turn your blogged book into a printed book or an e-book, all those readers, friends, tweeple, connections, listeners, and followers hopefully will run out and purchase it.

Angle Your Book for Success by Knowing Your Competition

Now we come to the Competing Books section of a book proposal. In the case of a blogged book and the proposal process, you now need to take a long, hard look at any other blogs that might compete with your blogged book. This helps ensure that you are the only one blogging on your topic or that you are blogging on the topic from a unique angle. You want your blog to be different from other blogs.

Keep your business hat on. You may, however, need to be ready to add in some of your writer's creativity, so have your writer's hat handy. (No more need for your social or public hat at this point; you can put it away.)

If lots of bloggers have chosen to write about your blogged book's topic, great! Don't be put off. That means readers find the subject interesting. Just as it is with printed books, if publishers keep publishing books on a certain topic, they must feel a market exists for those books.

On the other hand, you may find no one else blogging on your topic. That might prove a good thing—if anyone possesses an interest in reading about it. You can make a name for yourself as the first and only one in that particular market. For example, I began blogging about boys in the dance world from a mother's perspective. My mission was to mentor boys and help parents of boys who wanted to become professional dancers. No one else was writing about dance and boys in dance from this perspective. I gained a readership—and a pretty loyal one—pretty quickly at My Son Can Dance (http://mysoncandance.net). Additionally, when I began blogging a book about how to blog a book, no one else was doing this. I made a name and a place for myself in cyberspace on this topic. (That later became attractive to a publisher.)

If you find no other blogs on your topic, consider that this may be the case for good reason; no one may be interested in your topic. It's possible, though, that no blogs exist on the topic because no one has yet thought of your topic besides you.

If so, that's great! The market is just waiting for you. Buy a domain name that relates to your topic, set up your blog, and start writing and publishing fast! (More on how to do this in chapter five.) Then watch readers show up.

Since you are blogging a book, it behooves you to look not only at what other blogs out in cyberspace focus on your topic, but also at what books have been written on your topic. Make sure the book you are writing is different and adds something new to existing titles on bookstore shelves as well.

Also look at complementary titles. The exercise of looking for competing blogs relates to two sections of a book proposal: Competing *and* Complementary Titles. Complementary books are the related titles someone who is interested in your book might purchase as well; these books do not represent competition per se. If there are many books on one complementary topic, you might want to see if your book fits nicely with, or parallels, these books, since obviously a readership exists for them.

Don't forget to look at complementary blogs as well. These blogs might be great ones with which to try and develop reciprocal links at some point. The readers on a complementary blog might be just as likely to read your blog as the other—or to purchase your books, products, or services at a later date.

It's easy to find information on competing and complementary blogs. Simply go to blog catalogs, like Technorati.com or Blogcatalog.com, which offer listings of millions of blogs. Sometimes you can find a blog network related to a certain subject area. Try doing a Google search for Web or blog rings, blog networks, or blog directories on your topic. My blog, mysoncandance.net, is listed at Dance-Bloggers.com. If your blogged book involved a subject related to dance, you'd want to explore the blogs listed there. Another blog of mine, As the Spirit Moves Me (http://asthespiritmovesme.com), deals with both Jewish and secular spirituality, as well as human potential and personal growth issues; it is listed at JewPI. com under the "Blogs" category. If you were writing about Judaism, you'd want to check out the blogs at JewPI.com or at JewishBlogging.com. (As the Spirit Moves Me used to be listed there as well.)

Look at the ranking of the blogs you find in the catalogs. Each catalog will offer information on the popularity of a blog. Examine the highest ranked blogs as well as those lower down in the rankings.

Take all the information you gain from your research and take a second look at your blogged book idea in comparison to both the competing and complementary blogs and printed books. Ask yourself these questions:

- Does it still hold up? Is it unique?
- Does it need to be re-angled?
- Are you providing new benefits and features to blog readers who enjoy this subject?
- Do you need to rethink the content to make it stand out from the pack of other blogs or books?
- Will you choose to compete with the top-ranked published blogs or the ones ranked fifth, sixth, or even tenth? (You might find those lower down the scale an easier niche to break into.)

Be honest with yourself. This is your last chance to rethink, re-angle, and refocus your book's subject (and content) if you find your book is off base or has competition that is too similar. If necessary, make the changes to your idea now—before you start blogging—to ensure it truly fills a "hole" in the blogosphere and on the shelf of brick-and-mortar bookstores. Go back and redo your mind map and create a new pitch, overview, table of contents, and chapter-by-chapter synopsis. You might also need to rethink your markets. Taking these steps ensures your success in both the cyber and the traditional publishing marketplace.

Reggie Solomon did a great job of finding a niche in the blogosphere with both his blogs, Tomato Casual (TomatoCasual.com) and Urban Garden Casual (http://UrbanGardenCasual.com). He looked at what already existed in cyberspace and found a way to provide something a bit different—a casual approach to everything under the sun for tomato lovers and a casual approach to urban gardening.

What Resources Do You Need to Complete Your Blogged Book?

As you get closer to beginning to blog your book, consider this question: What resources do you need to complete your book? The answer to this question completes the section of a book proposal actually called "Resources Needed to Complete the Book."

This section may not seem to pertain to many blogged books, but I suggest you include the research for it as part of the proposal process. You, the blogger, may find you need little besides your mind, your fingers, a computer, and an Internet connection to write your book. Well, every blogger needs a little bit of money to pay for an Internet connection and a hosted website (since it's likely that you will eventually pay for a self-hosted blog—more on this in chapter five). You also need a computer.

Primarily this section does, indeed, cover costs. Here are the types of costs you might want to consider at this point in the process:

- PHOTOS—You might want to purchase a subscription to a stock photo provider, for example, or you might need a photographer for special needs.
- ART—You might need a logo or a series of cartoons to illustrate your book, or you might want to purchase a subscription to an online clip art service.
- PERMISSIONS—If you reproduce large sections of an existing book, you must purchase the rights from the publisher.
- HOSTING—If you don't already have a website, you will need this. (Or you can opt for a free hosted blog.)
- WEBSITE DESIGN—If you don't already have a website and you don't know how to create one, you may need to hire someone to create a website for you. You can use your free hosted or self-hosted blog as your website; however, even a self-hosted WordPress.org website may require that you hire someone to create an original design for your site.
- INTERNET CONNECTION—This will be the monthly charge for your Internet service.

In this section of a book proposal an aspiring author also declares how long it will take her to complete her book. So take a moment—or a few—to give yourself some deadlines. How much will you write each day, week, or month, and when will you "turn in" your finished book? In other words, how many blog posts will you commit to writing each week, and how many will it take you to complete your book? Given those figures, when will you finish your blogged book? Write that down. Make that part of your business plan for your blogged book.

Why Are You the Best Person to Write This Book?

Are you the type of writer who feels sure you possess the expertise to write your book, or are you the type of writer who questions whether you are good enough to do so? Do you know you are the best person to author the book you have in mind, or do you wonder if someone better exists?

Either way, at this point in the proposal process you must now write down all the reasons why you, indeed, are the best person to write your blogged book. In a nonfiction book proposal, this section is called "About the Author." Sounds pretty simply, right?

It can prove simple—or hard. That depends upon you. To complete this exercise, write a biography of your expertise and experience in the third person. Include the most important facts first, such as anything that makes you the expert on your topic, your educational degrees (if they apply to the topic), work experience, and anything else you consider important to the subject at hand. Include all of your achievements. See this as your résumé in prose, but make sure it's written specifically for your book.

Obviously an aspiring author who wants a deal with a traditional publisher needs to create an "About the Author" section for inclusion in a nonfiction proposal. However, a blogger needs a biography as well. Every blog should include an "About" or "About the Author" page. This allows readers to find out who you are and why you have the expertise to write your blog. This information gives your blog credibility.

So write your bio as part of the proposal process, and then copy and paste it on the "About" page of your blog. If you prefer to use a less formal bio for your blog, write it in the first-person tense using *I*. If you write your blog in a more formal voice, though, stick to third person for your bio as well.

Are You on a Mission?

If you decide to write a book proposal, you might want to include a mission statement after your author's bio. You've already worked on that. Remember that question I asked in chapter 3: "Why do you want to blog a book?" Remember the other ones I asked as well, including "What's your purpose?" "What's your mission?" and "What do you want to accomplish by writing this book?" The answers to those questions pertain here.

Not every book on writing a book proposal includes the Mission section; in fact, most don't. It's a fairly new section. However, my mentor and friend, Mike Larsen, who wrote *How to Write a Book Proposal,* asks his authors to include a mission statement, and such a section also appears in his own book. I find it a really important question to answer.

I'll reiterate: Knowing why you must blog or write this book will help you focus your energy on this project. It will help you clarify your reasons for blogging your book. It will help you decide if you *must* blog this book, and it will help the people considering purchasing your book (publishers and readers) decide if they *must* do so—if they *must* read it.

You can publish your mission statement on a page on your blog, too. It will let your blogged book readers know why you feel compelled to write this blogged book. In this way you allow them to buy into your mission as well.

Creating a Platform for You and Your Blog

The publishing world has changed dramatically over the last decade. No longer can you simply present an agent or a publisher with a good idea and good writing and expect to get a contract in return. You must prove you are a good business partner. This means you have laid the groundwork for selling your book by creating an author's platform. You have done what it takes to have prospective readers ready and waiting to purchase your book as soon as the publisher releases it.

Platform equates to how many people you know or who know you, and who will potentially buy your book. These people can be followers on Facebook, tweeple on Twitter, connections on LinkedIn, blog subscribers or readers, newsletter subscribers, podcast listeners, people reached via magazines, e-zines, and online publications for which you write, attendees at your talks and workshops, publicity partners, and fellow members of online and off-line associations. You build a platform through speaking, writing, social media activities, networking, and media gigs. You must build a platform before they will come—*they* meaning agents and publishers.

In today's publishing world the most important parts of a book proposal are the Promotion section and the Platform sections. Both show the publisher that you will help sell your book. They want a business partner, not just a writer. Do you have your business hat on?

Why do you, a blogger or the writer of a blogged book, care about platform or the Platform section of a book proposal? First, if you want your blogged book to be discovered and turned into a printed book by a publishing house, you need blog readers. Blog readers = platform (if enough of them exist). Second, if you would like to write another traditional book, or you plan on expanding your blogged book into a longer and more in-depth printed version, then your blog serves as a way to promote that book and to build platform (i.e., potential buyers).

Either way, the more you build platform via guest blog posts on other blogs, articles published on your topic, news releases, press releases, e-zine articles, media appearances, talks, workshops, and, of course, a steady flow of blog posts, the more readers will show up at your blog. All of these efforts become platform elements.

The Platform section of your book proposal—if you were to write one—would include a list of all the things you have done to date to develop an author platform. It would include statistics, such as how many unique visitors read your blog each day, how many page views you get daily on your website, how many places you have spoken in the last year or six months (and how many you have scheduled for the next six to twelve months), where you have appeared as a guest blogger, how many followers you have on Facebook, how many tweeple you have on Twitter, how many connections you have on LinkedIn, and how many people are on your mailing list.

Even if you don't write an actual proposal, it's a great idea to list these activities and statistics so you remember what you've done. It's also a good idea to keep track of these statistics so you can tell whether your readership and platform grow. Keep working on building your platform; don't let a month go by when you don't have some type of platform-building activity scheduled. In fact, you should do something to build platform every day.

By the way, the Platform section of a proposal can make or break an aspiring author's chance of getting a publishing deal. It's that important. So if your platform section lacks entries, you'll want to begin working on it ASAP. Here are a few things you can do to build your platform quickly:

- Spend time every day on social networking activities.
- Begin speaking to groups interested in your subject matter.
- Join groups interested in your subject matter—or any groups (professional, networking, social). And get involved—volunteer and take on leadership roles.
- Write articles on your topic for online and print publications.
- Begin pitching to the media. Subscribe to HelpAReporter.com, PitchRate. com, and ReporterConnection.com and respond to the journalists' queries you will receive.

Since I've now covered all the sections included in the Introduction of a nonfiction proposal, it's time to move on to the Outline.

PLANNING YOUR POSTS OR CONTENTS IN SCREEN-SIZED PIECES

At this point in the planning process, you know what your blogged book is about and you've outlined its features and benefits. You know who is going to read it and in what markets you will promote it. You know the competition and how to differentiate your blogged book from other blogs and books on the market already. You're now ready to consider the contents of your book.

However, a blogged book must follow the guidelines of a blog. No long chapters here, only short 250- to 500-word posts. Most blog visitors only want to read approximately one computer screen's worth of copy.

Therefore your task involves coming up with what in book proposal terms is called the "List of Chapters." This equates to the table of contents for your book and is the first of two sections included in the Outline of the proposal. However, you should have completed this in chapter three, after the mind mapping exercise. If not, you can do it now with a mind mapping exercise like the one described previously or by brainstorming your topic.

Once you have your table of contents, chunk the chapters down into screen-sized pieces comprised of all the subjects you came up with during your mind mapping. You also can accomplish this task or come up with more blog topics by brainstorming with other people, doing research, or simply attempting another brain dump to create a lengthy outline. Basically you want to break each chapter into numerous smaller sections consisting of subtopics with subheads. These actually serve as the titles to blog posts. Simply think about all the different topics you will cover in each chapter and give them titles; list them under the chapter title. (More on this exercise in chapter six.) These will each become a blog post in your blogged book.

To ensure you remember exactly what you are supposed to write when the time comes to compose those posts, take the time now also to write Chapter Summaries, the second and last section of the nonfiction book proposal. This entails composing a short but detailed chapter-by-chapter synopsis. I suggest you also write a brief summary of each post, even if it's just one or two sentences. This will serve not only as a reminder (it's not unusual after a month or two to have forgotten what you had in mind for many of your posts), but also as a basic outline for each post. If you feel the title of the post (the subhead) will be enough of a reminder, go with it; in many cases, that was enough for me.

Wow! Great job! You've completed the proposal process and compiled all the information you need for your blogged book's business plan or book proposal. Also, with your Overview, your List of Chapters and your Chapter Summaries in hand, you have the best writing guide possible.

Before you can begin blogging your book, however, you need a blog. It's time to create your blog so your book has a publishing home in cyberspace.

CHAPTER 5:

CREATING YOUR BLOG

To begin writing and publishing the content of your book on the Internet, you must first create a website where your book will "live." The type of website you need is called a blog. Some people think of blogs as something other than "real" websites. In truth, blogs are very real but they do operate a bit differently from traditional websites. (Sometimes they look different, too, and other times you can't tell the difference between a blog and a traditional website.) Better yet, some are free and all of them are relatively easy to use.

If you already have a website, you may consider including a self-hosted blog on that website. Most writers need a webmaster to set up a website and a self-hosted blog because it can be a complicated process. If you are technologically savvy, you may be able to do it yourself. With the right software, you can probably do the maintenance on your website and run your blog. My webmaster set up my websites and blogs, and, for the most part, I do all the maintenance myself.

In my experience, many writers are a bit (if not more) technophobic. Plus, they don't want to be anything but writers. They definitely don't want to take the time to become webmasters. Therefore, using a blog platform that doubles as a website offers a perfect solution for many writers, whether they are first venturing into the world of blogging and website maintenance or have experience doing so. These days, many people have websites created with WordPress technology. These are easy to use and maintain if you know how to blog.

A typical blog functions as a system for managing your content—the same as a website—as well as offering you an address, or home for that website, in cyberspace. It's an easy way to have control over your website. You can log in and add posts, pages, images, videos, and audio on your own without the need to pay a webmaster.

I'm not particularly technologically savvy. If I can manage a blog, so can you. You can create one, too. Even a technological delinquent like me can create a free hosted blog. I've done it several times, and it was reasonably easy to do.

HOSTED VS. SELF-HOSTED? THAT IS THE QUESTION

If you don't understand the difference between WordPress.com hosted blogs and WordPress.org self-hosted blogs, let me explain. (This explanation pertains to any type of hosted vs. self-hosted blog; I am using WordPress as an example because this is the most commonly used blogging platform.) WordPress.com, like other free blogging platforms, hosts your blog like a hosting company hosts your website. *Hosted* means the files and software used to build your website have somewhere to live on the Internet, and you don't need to worry about maintaining the software that runs your blog. WordPress.com hosts blogs for millions of people. As the blogger, you are in control of the content, but your site resides at the WordPress location. That means that the traffic you generate—the readers who show up to read your blogged book—show up at YourBloggedBook.WordPress.com, for example. Having a hosted blog with any blogging platform is a bit like housing it in a commune or an apartment building. Everyone shares the same address.

WordPress.org, on the other hand, is free software you download and install on your own Web host. You pay for hosting from a hosting company of your choice, such as GoDaddy.com or HostGator.com, but your blog lives at the location you choose at a specific address on the Internet that you and you alone host. Your blog or website is the sole tenant living at that residence. No other blog has the same address.

I've had free hosted blogs both on Blogger.com and on WordPress.com. Other free hosted blogging companies exist, such as TypePad.com; check them out as well, if you like. WordPress has become the most widely used and accepted blogging platform.

I prefer WordPress. In my experience, it offers more options and gives you more exposure. I immediately had more traffic to my blog when I switched to Word-Press.com from Blogger.com, and I could actually find my blog when I searched for it on Google. I couldn't find my Blogger.com blog when I searched for it, which doesn't make a lot of sense since Blogger.com is part of Google. Google's chief of search engine results, Matt Cutts, recommends WordPress. Enough said!

I also have several self-hosted blogs—five in all—with WordPress.org, which my webmaster set up for me. All but two of them began as free hosted WordPress. com blogs. (Notice the difference: WordPress.com = free and hosted by Word-Press; WordPress.org = fee-based and self-hosted by you.) In the last two years, my webmaster converted all my free hosted blogs to self-hosted blogs. It's best to start out hosting your own blogs because it saves you the trouble and the expense of converting to self-hosted blogs later. It also saves you the decision of what to do with the old free hosted blogs after you convert them to self-hosted blogs. Word-Press.com lets you delete them, make them private, or forward the old address to a new one. I didn't want to just delete mine because this can sometimes cause problems with the new hosted blog. I didn't want to make them private because they remain visible on the Internet for readers to find; plus, those who do find them get a message saying they are private. I didn't want to leave them up and running, although that's what ended up happening until I realized they were taking traffic away from my self-hosted WordPress.org blogs and that readers were still leaving comments there. Now I pay $12 per year to have the old hosted WordPress.com blog addresses forwarded to my new self-hosted WordPress.org addresses. (If I could do it over again, I'd start with self-hosted blogs and save myself that $36 per year I now pay in forwarding fees for three blogs.)

If you can't afford to self-host your blog, however, the free hosted ones work well until you're ready to convert—or forever if you so choose. Self-hosted blogs do offer you more options and visibility, plus they ensure that the traffic you garner goes to your website and not to someone else's website. Some of the better website hosting companies will allow you to host more than one site (blog) on one plan for just a few cents more each month.

If you don't know anything about hosting or about HTML codes (and you don't want to learn), you may want to stick with a hosted blog. Self-hosting your own installation of any blogging software may provide you with additional flexibility, but this only benefits you if you are willing to learn how to use it or if you can afford a webmaster to at least set it up for you. Then you can just write, post, and do simple maintenance.

Once the blog is designed and hosted, you can manage it yourself. I promise. Many website hosting companies offer the option to start with WordPress-hosted sites, thereby eliminating the need for installations of any kind, though you will still have to maintain the WordPress software by installing updates from time to time. Usually the updating process is as simple as the click of a button.

The process of setting up a free hosted blog is fairly self-explanatory. If you are having trouble with either a free hosted blog or a self-hosted blog, I suggest you hire a webmaster or blogging professional to help you. If possible, find one that offers online tutorials in the blogging platform you have chosen.

You can find more information on blog construction in some great books now on the market. You might try:

1. *Blogging for Dummies* by Susannah Gardner and Shane Birley
2. *The Complete Idiot's Guide to Creating a Web Page & Blog* by Paul McFedries
3. *WordPress for Dummies* by Lisa Sabin-Wilson and Matt Mullenweg

The hosted blog sites lead you through the process fairly effortlessly. However, I will discuss several steps to setting up your blog.

PURCHASE A DOMAIN NAME

Whether or not you plan on having a self-hosted blog, you should purchase a domain name for your blogged book. Your blogged book's domain name is its address in cyberspace. Should you convert from a free hosted blog to a self-hosted one, you'll need a domain name. (You may want to forward your old hosted blog to the new self-hosted blog's address, as I did.) If you begin with a self-hosted blog, you'll need it to get started. Purchase the exact same domain name as the title of your blogged book.

While you're at it, purchase a domain name that reflects your own name as an author. For example, I own ninaamir.com as well as howtoblogabook. com. You can direct this domain name to your blogged book's website. People who don't know the name of your blogged book (or who have forgotten it) may search for you by name and find your blog in this manner. Or you may want to create an author's website at some point in time; having the domain name (and ensuring that someone else doesn't purchase it) will come in handy. You might even purchase the domain name that reflects a character, place, unique phrase, or new brand you have created that exists only in your book. Consider also buying domain names that reflect other search terms that might direct readers to your blogged book. For example, I could purchase blogtobooksuccess.com.

If you can't get a .com name (e.g., howtoblogabook.com), get a .net name (e.g., howtoblogabook.net). These are the second most common type of domain name. If you can't get one of these two, pick one of the others, such as .info, .org, or .tv, or even .me. Some people purchase every domain name possible so no one else will purchase them. This becomes a bit costly, since each domain name has a yearly fee attached to it.

You can purchase domain names in any number of places. The cost varies, so do your research. Many places, like GoDaddy.com, offer cheap rates and hosting as well. You can do a Google search and then comparison shop or ask someone savvy about websites for advice.

CHOOSING A THEME

The way your blog, website, or blogged book looks depends upon the theme you choose. When you sign up for a free hosted blog, you can simply begin searching through the numerous themes offered and download one. Find the "Theme" option under the "Appearance" menu in the dashboard on WordPress.com. The same holds true for a WordPress self-hosted blog. Additionally, you can find more free—and not free—themes on various Internet sites. Simply Google "WordPress themes" or "free WordPress themes" to find them. First check out WordPress.org to find about one thousand or so freely available themes. You are likely to discover something that suits you and your needs there. (The direct address is http://wordpress.org/extend/themes/.)

I find choosing a theme the most time-consuming part of setting up a new blog. There are so many from which to choose! And they don't all work the same way. Some are search engine optimized; some are not. Some are widget ready; some are not. Some are complicated; some are simple. Some are pretty; some are ugly. Some are interesting; some are boring. A blog theme exists for every blogger's personality, that's for sure. I've been known to download one and think it's perfect only to discover it is too difficult for me to use or it has one strange hitch I dislike. That sends me back to search for a new theme all over again.

If you find that choosing a theme sends you over the edge, you may simply be overthinking your theme decision. Someone recently told me good blog content always outweighs blog design. Take a deep breath, and take a break. Then pick one of the themes you've tested out and use it for a while. You can always try another one later on.

If you can't see doing any or all of this yourself, there is another way to design your blog, website, and blogged book. You can hire a WordPress expert to design your theme. This takes only as long as the time needed to describe your blogged book, how you envision your blog and website, how many pages you need, and other basics. While you go off and begin writing the first posts to your blogged book, the designer will create your blog. You then need only write a check. The advantage to this method, which I must admit I have only employed once and for a very simple blog, is that your blog, website, and blogged book are unique. No one but you will ever have this blog design.

In any event, don't let your difficulty choosing a template keep you from getting started. In the beginning, nobody is reading or searching for your blogged book anyway. Use the default template if you must and make changes to the theme later when you have more experience blogging and some readers.

MANAGING YOUR BLOG MENUS

Your blog will have a lot of different menus. I'm not going to discuss all of them, but I will mention a few important ones.

First, let's focus upon the "Settings" menu. In this area you will give your blogged book its title and subtitle and ensure that its URL, or domain name, is correct, and your name and contact information are all displayed correctly.

Sticking again with the WordPress blogging program, under Settings, click on "General." There you will see a place to fill in your "Site Title." This is your blogged book's title. Underneath this, fill in the blank for "Tagline" with your subtitle. This then appears on the blog. In some cases your subtitle may be too long and will not look good in the blog's theme. You may need to pick another theme or shorten the subtitle for use on the blog.

Next, in the space for "WordPress Address" and "Site Address," add your domain name without www before it. For example, http://mybloggedbook.com.

Fill in the "Email Address" space with whatever e-mail address you want to use. Comments will go to this address.

Now go to the "Discussions" menu under Settings, and under "Default Article Settings" choose "Allow link notifications from other blogs (pingbacks and trackbacks)" and "Allow people to post comments on new articles." This means you will be notified if other bloggers mention your blog posts, and your readers can comment on your posts. In the following section, "Other Comment Settings," choose "Comment author must fill out name and e-mail," and "Enable threaded (nested) comments __ levels deep." This means you've asked those readers who want to comment to leave a name and e-mail address, so you know who they are and can contact them. And you've enabled a stream of comments to form on one post.

If you want to be notified when readers comment, in the next section, "Email me whenever," choose "Anyone posts a comment." You can also choose to be notified if a comment is held for moderation. Whether or not you must moderate all comments is up to you as well. Choose this in the next section, "Before a comment appears." Only adjust "Comment moderation" if you feel you have specific spam concerns.

Last, under the "Privacy" menu, which also resides under "Settings," be sure to click on the option "I would like my site visible to everyone including search engines and archives." This makes it possible for your blogged book to be found on Google, Yahoo, Bing, etc.

The rest of the general settings area should be self-explanatory.

Now go to the "Users" menu, and under that heading click on "Your Profile." Here you want to be sure to write in "admin" in the blank for "Username"—you are the administrator of the blog—and to type in your name or whatever name you choose in the blank for "Nickname." I suggest you use your first or first and last name for this so when you reply to a blog comment, readers will know it's you, the author of the blogged book.

When it comes to writing, WordPress allows you to create what it calls "authors." This helps you distinguish your blogging tasks. If you don't want to do maintenance on your blog, for instance, you may want an author login and password rather than (or in addition to) an administrator login and password. You can then log in with this and write like a mad thing and not have to worry about anything else going on with the website or blog. You won't be distracted from doing what you should be doing—writing. You can leave website or blog maintenance to someone else if you have a webmaster or blog expert doing this for you. Or you can log in as the administrator at any time to do something other than write.

Having an author and an administrator account also is considered a good security practice because websites can be accessed by other people, or "hacked." Passwords on administration accounts can sometimes be weak. Don't just use a form of the word "administrator."

Under "Display Name Publicly," be sure to choose how you want your name displayed. Also you can add a website, if you have one other than the blog itself, and fill in the other form fields, including a short bio.

CHOOSING PLUG-INS AND WIDGETS

Once you have your blog set up, you can choose from all sorts of fancy and not-so-fancy widgets and plug-ins. These add tools and features such as search boxes, archives, search engine optimization, backup tools, and ways to "ping" your posts to social networking sites and garner subscribers to your site, all via your blog. You can pick and choose which ones you like and want to use.

Widgets, which tend to be items added to the sidebar of your blog, are easy to add and remove. Plug-ins, additional blog features, are pretty easy as well if you know what to download. (You can also search for them even if you don't know the exact name of a particular widget.) Widgets are found under the Appearance menu. Plug-ins are a stand-alone menu.

If you can imagine some sort of handy dandy tool that would serve your blogged book, there is a good bet someone has created a widget that will do it for you. When searching for widgets and plug-ins, look at their ratings to judge their effectiveness. Choose wisely. Remember when you apply a widget and/or a plug-in, it may change your theme. Not all widgets and plug-ins are compatible with all themes. I added one to howtoblogabook.com that I use on all my other blogs, and it produced four lines of odd coding; I had to deactivate it. Then I added another and deactivated it as well and found my blog was suddenly "unavailable" because I hadn't removed the inactive plug-in. (Don't panic if something like this happens. Do some research on Google. Inevitably someone else has had the same experience and solved the problem.)

The most important widgets to add to a blog are:

- LINKS (such as a blogroll—blogs you recommend—or links to resources)
- ARCHIVES (sorted by month/date/year, depending upon which archive widget you get, of all your past posts)
- CATEGORIES (under which you file your posts)
- SUBSCRIBE (a tool that allows readers to subscribe to your posts by e-mail or RSS feed, such as with FeedBurner.com)

The most important plug-ins to add are:

- ALL IN ONE SEO (allows you to write a short description of your post and add keywords and phrases to help search engine optimization)
- SHAREWARE (such as AddtoAny: Share/Bookmark/E-mail Buttons, Sexy-Bookmarks, Socialize, or WP Social Toolbar so readers can share, bookmark,

and e-mail your posts and pages using any service, such as Facebook, Twitter, Google, StumbleUpon, Digg, and many more.)

- **AKISMET** (comes with your WordPress install, but be sure to set up an account on the Akismet website to activate this "captcha" plugin and to protect your blog from comment and trackback spam; you might need a better captcha plugin later as you get more traffic.)
- **GOOGLE XML SITEMAPS** (generates a special XML sitemap which helps search engines like Google, Yahoo, Bing, and Ask.com to better index your blog)
- **ULTIMATE GOOGLE ANALYTICS** (enables Google Analytics on your blog)
- **WP-DBManager** (manages and schedules backup of your WordPress database)
- **DISQUS** (a comment moderation system that replaces WordPress's built-in comment moderation system with a more widely accessible comment feature set; offers a remote comment system that allows you to log in using social networks, like Facebook, Twitter, etc.)
- **WP-CACHE** (recommended for sites that get a lot of traffic to speed up downloading time for your readers)

INSTALLING ANALYTICS

One of the most important tools you want to add to your site is an analytics program. The free hosted WordPress.com sites have basic analytics. This allows you to see how much traffic comes to your blog, what type of search terms are being used, and what pages people are visiting.

For self-hosted blogs, choose from any number of free analytics available, such as Site Meter or Google Analytics. Your hosting company may also have analytics (free or fee based). Sometimes I use more than one type. Try out programs like WassUp, another free plug-in, which will not count the bots, crawlers, and spiders (automated processes used by search engines) that visit the blog if you request. This way, you can tell how many actual visitors showed up to read what you wrote.

Once you have analytics on your blog, you can tell how many readers are visiting your site. It won't be as many as you would like, especially at first. Educate yourself on the difference between a *hit*, a *visitor*, a *unique visitor*, and a *page view*. I'm going to spend some time on this, because most people do not understand it. As a blogger and author of a blogged book, you *need* to understand it (even if you really don't *want* to understand it) so you can talk about your blog statistics in an educated manner. Why? So you can tell an agent or acquisitions editor about your platform and provide the correct statistics when they ask—which they did when I was negotiating my contract for this book. I had offered hits in my proposal because this is the largest number. (I knew it wasn't the most important.) Later, after the proposal was accepted and we were negotiating the contract, the sales and marketing team asked me for unique visitors and page views because these are the numbers that really matter. So, here we go. (Don't let your eyes glaze over.)

Technically a *hit* is each file sent to a browser by a Web server; therefore, it's not a visitor, or reader, of any type. It's anything on the page of your blogged book that gets sent to a browser—a photo, content, a logo, a post.

A visitor is a browser that accepts a *cookie*, or small script. Let's say you visit a website. A cookie then is placed on the hard drive of your computer by the server of that website. The cookie is used to recognize your specific browser/computer combination if you to return to the same site. If a cookie is not accepted, an IP number or address, which is like an online fingerprint, will track your browser/computer combination. Each Internet connection has its own IP number or address; an IP number or address is a bit like your home address in cyberspace. IP addresses on any network are a single device, but they can be a single IP address shared by a number of computers. Therefore, a single IP address in your website log may not represent just one person.

A visitor could be an actual reader or a crawler, spider, or bot—all of those "things" that come from the search engines to catalog websites and content.

The all-important unique visitor refers to an actual unduplicated person—not bots, crawlers, or spiders (and not a hit)—to your website over the course of a specified time period—twenty-four hours. Different from a site's hits or page views, which are measured by the number of files requested from a particular site, unique visitors are recognized and measured by cookies they accepted previously (unbeknownst to them) and by their unique IP addresses. Also, they are counted only once no matter how many times they visit the site during that time period—unless they deleted the cookie off their computer and then return to the site. In this case, they will get a new cookie and be counted again. Thus, in simple terms, a unique visitor is someone who visits your site once in a given time period.

A visit occurs when someone or something (possibly a bot) visits your site. It consists of one or more page views or hits. One visitor can generate multiple site visits.

"Page views" are generated each time a visitor views a page on your website, regardless of how many hits are created at the same time. Pages are comprised of files, and every image in a page is a separate file. Readers look at a blogged book page, or a blog post, thus creating a page view. They may see numerous images, graphics, pictures, and all of these generate multiple hits. One page view can create hundreds of hits, which is why page views are more important than hits.

Now that you understand how to tell if you have actually had readers to your blogged book, it's time to start creating something for people to read. This gives them a reason to come to your website or blog. Then you can watch your analytics, which basically means waiting for readers to arrive. As you keep writing, you'll be able to watch the numbers grow.

YOU NEED PAGES

Before you begin writing your blogged book, I suggest you take a little time to create some additional pages on your blog besides the actual blog page. This becomes especially important if you plan to use your blog as your website. In other words, if you don't have your blog self-hosted on an actual website and it serves as your website, you will want to add pages in addition to those that feature the actual blogged book.

Pages are easy to add in WordPress.com or Wordpres.org. On the left side of your blog dashboard you'll see a menu that says "Pages." Underneath this, the menu has an option to "Add new." Simply click on this. You will then be given a menu to add a new page.

Title the first new page you add "About the Author." (If you took the time to go through the proposal process in chapter four, you have already created a bio and you can use it here.) Since you are writing a book, you want readers to know the author. In particular, you want acquisitions editors and literary agents who drop by to know who you are. Be sure you write your author's bio in a professional manner. I like the ones written in the third person, just like in a book proposal. However, if you are writing your book in an informal tone, you might want to write your bio in the first person. Lots of blogs have witty and informal "About" or "About the Author" pages, but they aren't blogging a book. Include a professionally taken photo as well.

Next create an "About This Blog" page. Tell your readers why you began writing your blog. Consider including the mission statement, or part or all of the Overview that you wrote during the proposal process in chapter four as well, especially the part about the benefits of reading the blogged book. Let your readers know why you feel compelled to write your blogged book and what they will gain by becoming loyal blog followers. Help them buy into your blog.

You may want to include a "Media Kit" page. On this page include a shorter bio with a link to a longer bio, a downloadable photo, topics upon which you can speak, and links to questions the media can ask you on your topic. If you already speak on your topic (and you should), you can list the names of your speeches. You may also want a page specifically dedicated to your speaking activities—such as a "Hire Me to Speak" page. There you can list upcoming and past speaking engagements.

Include a "Contact Me" page with contact information as well. If you offer services of some sort or sell anything, you can add "Products and Services" pages.

You can add as many pages as you like, or as many as the theme you have chosen will permit, but be sure that if they are listed underneath the banner at the top of the home page of the blog you don't end up with so many that you run out of space. The most important pages to include are those that pertain to you, the author, and your blogged book. Second in importance are your media or speaking pages, so be sure that information has been included as well. Whatever doesn't fit at the top of the blog page can be added on the sidebar depending upon your theme.

If your blog is self-hosted on a website, many, if not all, of these pages can be included on your website rather than on the blog itself.

Finally, you are ready to begin writing your blogged book one post at a time in cyberspace.

CHAPTER 6:

WRITING YOUR BLOGGED BOOK

Okay! Let's start writing that blogged book!

Writing a blogged book is a bit different from writing a manuscript for a printed book because blogging lends itself to informality, brevity, and immediacy. When blogging, you can write, in short bits and pieces as if composing an e-mail to a friend. You don't ponder over your writing for days and weeks; you write, edit, and publish. The whole process is quick, and the whole book manuscript comes together quickly.

Blogs began as live journals, and many people considered them streams of consciousness—simply unedited thoughts thrown together and published. I'm not suggesting you go to that extreme with your book. You want to carefully choose your words and edit your copy before you send your posts into cyberspace. You want to put your best words forward—up to a point. You don't want to become a perfectionist or this will deter you from publishing posts frequently.

Consider your blogged book your first or second draft. Don't get upset if you discover you have gotten off track, left something out, made a mistake, or need to change, add, or delete copy. It's true, this happens for all of cyberspace to see (assuming you have blogged book readers). You do, indeed, make your errors and foibles in public.

However, if you don't stumble too often, it isn't a problem. Plus, you can avoid this issue for the most part by planning out your book well (see chapter three) and working on your blog copy off line prior to publishing posts, a process that I'll cover later in this chapter. Blogging software makes it easy to go back and edit posts, delete posts, and insert new posts into the "stream" of your book. Thus I don't consider errors much of a deterrent to blogging a book since you can correct most of them once you discover them.

Remember, you can think of your blogged book as a test-market version of your printed book. Know that before the printed book gets published you will have another chance to edit, revise, and add to it—to create a final draft. This version does not have to be perfect, and hopefully you'll find that fact to be creatively freeing. It's simply about getting your thoughts down quickly, in short bursts, on a regular schedule without the need for perfection.

While you compose your book, keep in mind that you are blogging. The beauty of blogging lies in the fact that it allows you to write about what's in your heart or mind at any moment or on any particular day. As you blog your book, you may find yourself going off on a tangent. Perhaps you feel moved to write about something related to your topic that's not in your table of contents. Or maybe you decide to take a day or two to discuss something that simply feels important to you. That's okay. In fact, it's great. As you'll read in chapter ten, the bloggers mentioned there who received book contracts were all simply blogging. None of them set out to blog a book. Their books were organic products of good blogging. So, first and foremost, be a good blogger. However, set out with a plan. Know where you are going and want to end up. This way you'll produce the content you need for your book—and hopefully some extra content as well.

I set up Google Alerts on subjects related to my book. (You can easily do this by going to Google and looking under its menus or typing "alert" into the Google search engine and then following directions.) I received daily notification about things like blog-to-book deals or industry studies related to blogging and blogs turned into books. These affected what I wrote about in many cases, often inspiring me to blog on new subjects that were not on my already lengthy list of planned subjects for my book.

Sometimes in the midst of writing, another idea would come to me or I'd realize I had totally forgotten about an important step in the book-blogging process. I would then write that blog post. If I realized this step needed to be inserted earlier in the book, I would move it to the appropriate "date," or I would just let my readers know it should have come earlier in the book (or several days earlier in the blog).

Occasionally I offered a "commercial break." If I had a workshop or telesminar coming up, I'd actually tell my readers about it in a blog post as well.

As with any writing process, I didn't stay tethered to my outline. I let it be exactly that—an outline. I stayed pretty close to its boundaries, but the outline grew and changed as I wrote.

Feel free to write—to blog! Don't ever let the book blogging become a constraint. Allow it to open your creative flow.

CREATING YOUR BLOGGED BOOK CONTENT

Hopefully you took the time in chapter four to create your List of Chapters (table of contents) and to write your Chapter Summaries, a chapter-by-chapter synopsis. If not, I suggest you do so now. This provides a starting point for any book. Remember, you are, indeed, writing a book even if you intend to blog it.

As I suggested in chapter four, break down each chapter's subject into as many subheads, or subtopics, as you can think of at this time. These become the different blog posts you will write, each one averaging about 250 to 500 words in length. If you were writing a full-length chapter for a printed book, you likely would break it up with subheads anyway. Most chapters have at least four or five subheadings. For a blogged book, you will need more. Depending upon the length of your chapter, you may need ten or twenty subheads (post titles). Write them as catchy titles someone will want to read. Lots of blogs include lists, such as "5 Ways to Skin a Cat" or "10 Tips for Success," or questions, such as "How Do I Use Twitter?" or "How Can I Land an Agent?"

Although you wrote many, if not all, of your chapter and post titles in chapter 4, now reconsider their titles as you think about how you will set up your blog Categories. Categories are used to catalog the subject of your posts and normally are listed in the sidebar of your blog so readers can find posts on particular topics. Will your categories be filed by chapter titles and subheadings? Or will you use subjects about which you have written? Subjects are better for SEO and simple for reader searches. Plus, your category listing could get quite long if you include every subhead you've used in each chapter. It's best to keep your category listing on the short side; some people say ten to fifteen topics. You can add subtopics within each category to divide topics further.

After you create your subheads (blog post titles), consider the content you want to include in each of these smaller chapter sections. Each blog post will be only about three or four paragraphs long.

One way to come up with both titles and content involves asking yourself five or ten questions that you answer in each chapter, or in parts of your chapter. The questions become blog post titles. You then provide the answers to these questions—your content—as you compose blog posts. When you edit your manuscript into a book, you either can change the questions into transition sentences that begin each paragraph or you can write an introduction to the section itself and delete the questions. (You'll probably need an introductory paragraph for each section anyway.) Some people use the questions as additional subheads. I don't prefer this approach, because I don't find it interesting to read a book full of questions and answers. The questions do work well as blog post titles, however, since search engines tend to like questions.

Another way to come up with a list of blog posts entails writing "keyword sentences" for topics under each of your chapter subheads. These can function like transitions between paragraphs in your posts, but primarily serve to remind you what to write about. You also might use keywords that search engines can find in these sentences (more on this later). Right now we are mainly concerned with words that focus you on the subject at hand when it's time to write your posts. Begin by writing a sentence that lets you and the reader know what topic will be covered, then elaborate upon it for the reader. You can do this with a full statement, with a few words, or by asking yourself questions; you can delete these writing prompts afterwards and simply make sure all copy flows well. This makes for much more interesting writing than including questions, as I mentioned before. If you wrote a strong keyword sentence that flowed well into your subsequent blog post, however, you can include it.

If you look at the previous paragraph, for example, you can see that the first sentence functions as a keyword sentence.

Another way to come up with a list of blog posts entails writing "keyword sentences" for topics under each of your chapter subheads. The rest of the paragraph elaborates upon this.

This keyword sentence also employs some search engine keywords and keyword phrases: blog, blog posts, writing, keyword sentences, keyword, chapter subheads, subheads, and topics.

If I had put a subhead on this section it might have read:

How to Use Keyword Sentences to Create Chapter Subheadings

As you write, you will surely think of other posts to add under your subheadings or subtopics. You may even add more subtopics with additional posts. As I blogged this book, I came up with many additional topics. Again, allow yourself to be a blogger and a writer. Add more content as the inspiration hits you. Hopefully you'll have days when you get in the flow and new topics come to mind. It's good to have a springboard from which to start, however.

As I began editing and revising, I added even more I felt I'd left out or had forgotten in the first draft. Keep in mind that as you blog your book you produce a *first draft*, not a final draft, of your book. Of course, you will polish each post as much as possible before you hit the publish button, but your blogged book will not be a perfect or finished version of your book. Remember that, and it should free you to write and publish quickly and easily. Don't let your Inner Perfectionist take hold of you and stop you from publishing your work on the Internet.

HOW TO COMPOSE YOUR BLOG POSTS

I suggest you compose your book as a manuscript written in Microsoft Word or some other word processing program and not on your blog program. In other words, don't write your book in WordPress, TypePad, or Blogger, then hit publish and consider this your manuscript. By creating an actual manuscript, you will have a version to later edit when it comes time to produce a printed book. Since you are producing a draft, when it comes time to work on that printed book, you will want to have a complete manuscript from which to work.

If you have not created a manuscript while blogging your book, you will then have to copy and paste all your posts off your blog to do so. And that's all you'll have on your actual blog—individual posts—not a continuous set of posts that can be copied as one long document. That's a *huge* job you want to avoid. Plus, a manuscript gives you a backup of your hard work. You blog should be providing a backup of all your posts (see the list of widgets in chapter five), but the more backups the better).

By creating a manuscript, you have the ability to see your book being created before your eyes in a more traditional manner as well. Here you can run a word count. You can move posts around if you find that the order isn't quite right. (You can also do this on your blog by changing the dates.) You can print out the document, and read a hard copy. You can even put it in a binder, place dividers between the chapters, and start getting the tangible and visual sense that you are, indeed, writing a book.

If you prefer, you can write your posts in your blogging software and then copy and paste them into Microsoft Word after publishing them. Some people feel more like bloggers if they write in their blogging program. Doing so also can give you a better sense of a "screen's worth of copy." It's pretty easy to preview your post and see how it looks on your computer screen, and this can feel fun and exciting.

A screen's worth of copy consists of a printed page's worth, or 250 words—more if you choose—of content. Some bloggers write 1,000-word posts if they only post once a week. This also is okay for what are called long-tail posts. These are much like evergreen articles, ones readers come back to again and again because the topics never get old or because people search for them on the Internet over and over again. These will drive traffic to your blog day and night even though you wrote them long ago. I wrote one like this for my blog, My Son Can Dance, on how to wear a dance belt. (You'd be amazed at how many people search for information on dance belts and how to wear them.) However, most of your posts should be within the 250- to 500-word range. You don't have to do a word count every time, but keep in mind that every 700-word post you write could be two days worth of posts rather than one. That's a pretty large incentive to break that post into two, if you ask me.

Like anything else you write, a post should have a beginning, a middle, and an end. In the case of blogging a book, though, this is all the more important because your posts, while part of the same book and the same chapter (or even the same section of a chapter) are published individually. The beginning also should have a hook or lead—an enticing first sentence that makes the reader want to continue reading.

Blogging a book and writing a book differ primarily in the fact that each post you publish must function as a stand-alone unit. You can link to earlier material you have published so your readers know what has come before, but a person reading one particular post may not have read previous posts. They may "pick up" your book at any point. In fact, a keyword search may point them to your blog at whatever page seems most pertinent to that search engine. For example, if someone searched for "why blog a book" on Google's search engine, they might find only this blog post of mine: "Why Blog a Book? You and Your Blog Might Get Discovered! (Part 9)." If they clicked on the link they would find themselves at part nine of a ten-part series of posts at the How to Blog a Book blog. They would, of course, have the option of clicking forward or back, turning the pages, if you will, of my blogged book to read the other posts on the topic.

Therefore, as you write your posts, you must first write them as complete entities. Then you must provide links to any other posts that might be pertinent to the material you cover. Additionally, you should create a flow from one post to the next to keep your readers turning pages—reading from one day to the next. You do this by teasing them on. You might, for instance, say, "Tomorrow I'll tell you all about how to write a blog post," or "In my next post, I'll explain how to schedule your posts so you don't have to write a post every day." This makes your readers want to come back for more.

When appropriate, you will want to add the words, "In yesterday's post I mentioned … " or "In my last post …," and then add in whatever you wrote about yesterday. Don't forget to also create a link (aka hyperlink) to yesterday's post with some of those words. This allows readers to flip the pages easily.

In the same way, if you mention a term you defined ten posts back, provide a link to that post. If you discussed an important concept, provide a link back to it. This provides continuity within your blogged book, which does not have an index or glossary. You could, I suppose, add a blog page with a glossary, but it's better to keep your readers reading pages in your book.

Know that as you continue writing in this manner you will create transition sentences at the beginning and the end of each post that you may or may not want in a printed book. Don't worry about that now. You need them for the blogged version of your book. You can (and must) edit them out later when you are getting ready to produce a printed book.

Using this basic post format, you now can begin writing. Start with your introduction or just jump right into chapter one. You can use the introduction in the "About This Blog" page if it works better there. In either case, chunk your book down to post-sized bits and keep them individualized but flowing one into the next. If you want to allow readers to go back to "page one" of your book, or the first post, so they can read from the beginning, you can create a page with a link to your very first post. That's what I did on the How to Blog a Book blog; I called it "Page #1."

BE CONVERSATIONAL

Even if you are blogging a book on a technical subject or on a scholarly topic, you can approach writing your book in a conversational manner. I suggest you try this, since most people who read blogs expect the author to "talk to them" in a chatty and relaxed manner.

However, if you feel you must maintain a professional tone, then by all means, choose that as the writing style of your blogged book. Only you know best what writing style will most effectively communicate your message.

Actually, your readers know best. You can ask them what they think or what they like. Try polling them. (You can add a poll plug-in to your blog easily.) Or simply ask readers to give you feedback via the comments function. At the end of a post ask: "Would you prefer that this blog be written in a more conversational and less formal tone?" See what types of comments you get back. Or write one post in a conversational tone and another in a formal tone, and ask for feedback.

If you aren't getting readers, which means you have no one to poll or to ask for comments, you can change your style and see if you attract readers that way. Maybe you need to stop thinking so much about your blog being a book and simply blog for a while. You can get back to blogging your book later. Keep your book's table of contents in mind but don't marry yourself to it. Allow yourself to write in a more free-flowing manner and see what happens. Or try including more keywords; this surely will attract more readers.

I had an interesting experience when I began editing this book. I had blogged it and then put the manuscript away for about six months after completing the book proposal. As I started editing and revising it I found myself quite taken with the voice I'd used. I really liked it! I found my blogging voice friendly and chatty, yet authoritative. It sounded and felt authentic to me and highly readable. In some of my other work, I find my writing much more verbose and formal. This writing was to the point while remaining warm.

Thinking back, I hadn't consciously decided to do anything differently when I sat down to blog this book. I was just aware of the fact that I was writing short pieces, and I needed to get them done quickly. In reality, the posts for How to Blog a Book were fit into and around the other work I was doing. I was working with my book-editing and coaching clients, writing monthly articles for a magazine, composing blog posts daily for one of my other blogs, and doing other jobs as well. In other words, I was busy and didn't have time to dawdle over these particular blog posts.

I had the same experience when I edited another short book of mine comprised of ten blog posts. The warm yet confident voice I used for that seemed to come from somewhere deep inside me. I had a friend proofread that manuscript and give me feedback, and she also enjoyed the tone of the writing more than some of my other work.

http://howtoblogabook.com

So allow yourself some freedom with your blogged book. No one is looking over your shoulder. You are your only boss. No one is telling you how to write this book or even what to write each day. No one knows if you are sticking to your chapter summaries or List of Chapters. There is no right or wrong way to blog it or write it. Express yourself in an honest and authentic manner. Let your passion, your voice, and your authenticity shine through. Let your readers get to know the real you. You'll be surprised what happens when you do.

In fact, that's the difference between a successful blog and an unsuccessful one. Successful blogs have at their helms bloggers who write with passion and purpose, who feel inspired and who every day show up as nothing less than their true selves with all their colors flying. Almost every blogger I interviewed who landed a book deal attributed his or her success to feeling passionate about the subject of the blog and being authentic while blogging. If you feel the need for inspiration, go read their blogs.

You'll be blogging long past the time you finish writing your book. If you ever find your passion, motivation, enthusiasm, or inspiration for blogging or for blogging your book waning, try these things:

- Read other blogs on your topic—and comment on them.
- Get involved in groups and forums on your subject.
- Read books on your topic.
- Set up Google Alerts on your topic or on additional keywords related to your topic (and be sure to open the alerts and read the pertinent posts).
- Ask some experts to write guest blog posts for you so you get a break.
- Take a brief blogging vacation (tell your readers you are, in fact, on vacation for two or three days).
- Do research on your topic.
- Talk to other people who are interested in your topic or who are experts in your subject area.
- Explore the possibility of using multimedia on your blog—audio and video.
- Interview experts in your subject area and post the information or the interview; you can even post it as an audio clip, podcast, or video.

- Videotape yourself talking about your subject matter or about the process of blogging a book, and post this as a way to let your readers get to know you.

USE KEYWORDS IN YOUR POSTS

One of the most important things to do when you write copy for the Internet involves using keywords. Remember, keywords and keyword phrases are the words on your site that match search terms. Search terms are the words and phrases that people looking for information on the Internet type into the search forms of search engines.

It's a great idea to think about all the keywords you might use while writing about your book. What words or phrases, for instance, relate to your topic? These are the keyword and keyword phrases you want to use over and over again.

As you do, they populate your blog, blogged book, and your website. They are then found by spiders, bots, and crawlers, or the programs that harvest information for search engines. The more keywords and keyword phrases on your pages, the higher your blog, blogged book, or website climbs in search engine results pages (SERPs). Also, the more often you post new content to your site, the more likely that these visitors will show up to index what is there. This also means that if you post often and use lots of great keywords and keyword phrases, your blog and blogged book will move up in the SERPs. Thus it will gain the coveted top ten Google ranking; when you search for your keyword or keyword phrase using Google's search engine, your blogged book will show up on the first page.

There is a lot more to SEO than this, but using keywords and keyword phrases well provides a start.

I want to caution you not to get fixated on the need to use keywords or try to build them into your blog posts as you write. Here's why: If you stay on topic, you naturally will use keywords in all your blog posts. You won't be able to avoid it. If you focus on using keywords, your writing will become stilted, and Google, for instance, may decide you are using "keyword spamming" techniques to raise your blog's ranking in SERPs. Keyword spamming is a technique by which you use many keywords related to your subject—as many as fifty—and try to pack them into your content regularly. Not only will Google and other search engines fault you for this, your readers will as well. It's best to choose ten to twenty keywords with which you want to work and use them when they fit organically into your writing.

I rarely bother to look up keywords for my blog topics. I know what they are; if I look them up, I do so simply to see if there are any I might not have thought of. Then I write about my topics day in and day out, and those keywords come up over and over again without me thinking about them. They are inherent to my writing if I stay on topic.

Here's the thing about SEO: It really comes down to great content. You can search out the best keywords for your topic and fill your content with those words but at a certain point the search engines discover what you are doing. And they don't like it. If you are on point when writing about your topic, you will write keyword-rich content without any extra effort on your part.

By simply being authentic and writing great content, your blog posts will search engine optimize themselves. You will write passionately about your topic and your copy will naturally include the words that attract readers and search engines.

This becomes even more true when blogging a book. Since you cover one topic for a long period of time, your posts contain many keywords. You write in an authentic manner and with an authentic voice. You do so passionately and from a place of personal or soul purpose or mission. In the process, you produce great content with superb SEO. At some point while you're blogging your book, your book should get noticed by the search engines and your ranking should increase on the SERPs.

It's a good thing to know what keywords and keyword phrases are most searched for on your topic. Create a list. Hang it up by your computer screen. Then forget about it.

COMPARING KEYWORDS AND WEBSITE RANKING

I am by no means an expert on SEO. I know just a little about SEO and evaluating competitive keywords. That said, maybe I know more than you. So let me tell you what I know.

One of the best free places to go to compare keywords is Google. You can find the "Google Adwords Keyword Tool" by typing those words into the Google search engine. Then plug in your word or phrase, and it will tell you how it ranks. The higher the ranking or number, the more people searching for that word or phrase. For example, when I plugged in "how to blog a book," the tool told me there were 823,000 global monthly searches and 301,000 local monthly searches. You also can gain access to paid keyword tools if you want to go to that expense. These might have more bells and whistles and offer additional information you may find useful.

Don't get too excited if your keywords prove to be most popular. You actually may not want to rely on the most-searched phrases because they probably already have sites or blogs that dominate them. Instead you might want to try to dominate less-used keywords and keyword phrases. You'll stand a better chance of working your way up to a top ten ranking on SERPs.

You can find out who leads the SERPs with your keywords by simply doing a search with those terms in any search engine. The top ten websites listed will be those with the most keywords or keyword phrases. Put the term in quotation marks and search again and you will get more accurate search results. Then see who is in line ahead of you.

Now that I have gotten in way over my head, I'm turning back to safe ground. Let's discuss how to schedule the writing of your blogged book—something I know a lot more about.

WRITING ON A SCHEDULE

When I suggest to aspiring authors, especially those in need of platform, that they create a blog, most tell me they don't want to blog. It's just one more thing "to do." In fact, writing a blog post every day or several times a week only represents an unwanted writing commitment, with a scheduled writing time and number of pages (in this case *posts*) to produce each day.

Authors publishing books one post at a time in cyberspace are no longer *aspiring authors*. They are *actual authors,* published writers. These authors write and publish. Like most working authors, they write every day … or *most* days. Or so it *seems*. Let me explain.

If you have other writing projects to keep up with on a daily basis or you hold down a full-time job, your blogged book can end up feeling like extra work. It can seem difficult to fit in time to write daily posts.

Believe me, I know that writing daily or even weekly posts can be hard. I have four blogs to keep up with on a regular basis, one of which requires three posts per week. When I started the How to Blog a Book blog, I already had three blogs, and I actually didn't plan to write another blog. The opportunity just presented itself, and I took it. I then had to keep up with the blog on a regular—meaning three or four times per week—basis until I completed blogging the book. And at that point I still needed to keep up with the blog to some extent. When November rolls around every year, I have to manage thirty full days of posts for my fifth blog, Write Nonfiction in November (http://writenonfictioninnovember.com).

When it comes to blogging a book, it's easy for me to say, "Remember, you are writing a book. Every aspiring author wants to write his book. So, make it a priority." In some cases, you'll still protest, "I just don't have time every day to write!"

I've got good news for you: Blogging a book offers a huge advantage over other ways to author a book—especially if you are short on time on a daily basis. First, you write short posts. Thus you do not have to make a lot of time to write. It does not take long to compose 250 words each day. That's all you need— 250 words. Write 500 words if you like, but that's plenty. Edit your copy once. Post it in your blog and proofread it in the "preview" mode. Make the necessary changes, and then hit "publish." If you write 250 words, the whole process might take you an hour, unless you are a slow writer. (You will have written just one page of copy.)

In this way, writing three to four posts a week, I wrote the core of this manuscript in five months. Blogging a book will help you commit to writing your book; it will help you commit to finding time to write your book. Commit to three posts a week minimum if you truly want to find time to write.

SCHEDULING YOUR BLOG POSTS TO PUBLISH LATER

If you feel you don't have time to commit to writing your book every day, here's another great advantage and a phenomenal feature of blogging a book: Most blogging software offers a way to write in advance and publish your posts on a schedule. This means you can sit down today, like I am doing, and knock out three to five posts, and then schedule them to publish at a later date, such as during the week.

Voilà! It looks like you've been writing three to five times during the week when actually you sat down and wrote for a few hours one day (or two), scheduled your posts, and walked away from your blogged book until next week or next month.

For example, when I began blogging How to Blog a Book, I wanted to publish three to five posts each week. I would often write a post and publish it on Monday and then immediately write two more posts in advance and schedule them to publish on Wednesday and Friday. That way, I knew I'd have at least three posts published in the coming week. I still had the freedom to write on the other days if I found the time.

For my blog Write Nonfiction in November, scheduling posts is a necessity. I publish thirty consecutive posts in one month, and most years I'm on vacation during the Thanksgiving holiday. Plus, at the same time, I'm trying to keep up with four other blogs, client work, and miscellaneous other projects (like writing books and promoting myself). I get as many posts as possible written, edited, and scheduled so the blog basically runs itself most of the month.

Scheduling your blog posts is simple. The function for scheduling posts in WordPress can be found just above the "Publish" button. (In most other blogging software programs it's in about the same place.) You'll find a prompt that says, "Publish immediately" with the option to "edit." Click on "edit," and you will discover that you can choose the time and date when you would like your post to publish. After you have done that, click on "okay," and "schedule." (Usually the "publish" button changes to "schedule" at this point. If it still says "publish," don't panic. You probably didn't click "Okay.")

Now go to "Posts" and "edit." You'll see the list of all your published and scheduled posts. Notice that the status of the post you just scheduled appears as "scheduled" rather than "published." If you had just published it, the status would tell you how long ago you had published the post. If you published it several days ago, it would just say "published."

KEEPING UP WITH YOUR BLOG WHEN USING THE SCHEDULING OPTION

As you've probably realized, scheduling your posts offers a definite advantage for the busy blogger or author. Now that you know how to schedule your blogged book's posts, however, you are at risk. You may walk away from your blogged book all week and pay no attention to what's going on there, such as how many readers have left comments. That's a definite disadvantage to scheduling your posts.

You want, therefore, to have one day a week when you actually write a live post—one you write and publish right then and there. This keeps things fresh. It allows you to comment on what's going on in the moment, such as news events that might affect your topic, comments that have just come in, or events in your life. It ensures that your blogged book stays fresh and alive.

If you have a time-sensitive blogged book, you may not be able to use the scheduling option often or at all. It's nice to know it's there, though, should you need it.

As I mentioned, I tend to schedule a few posts each week and then write a few live posts. Actually, in the first three months of blogging How to Blog a Book (February through April), I wrote almost all the blogs live. That explains the long gaps between some blogs. If you read my other blog, Write Nonfiction NOW!, you'll notice that on some days posts don't show up until really late in the day—late especially if you live on the East Coast. That's because I may have had such a busy day that I didn't get around to writing my post until the evening. I tend to write every one of those posts live, and I write three days a week. (For the first eleven months, I wrote five days a week.) You can avoid these kinds of issues by using the scheduling function and writing ahead in conjunction with writing live posts on the days you know you can schedule in time to blog your book in real time.

If you don't choose to write a live post at some point during week (besides the one you post just after your weekly writing period), be sure to show up and check out what's happening in terms of comments. Hopefully, your readers find your posts interesting enough to actually comment upon them. If so, you should be replying to those comments. And you should do that on a timely basis. (I'll tell you more about how to interact with readers' comments later in this chapter.)

If you've used the scheduling option, you'll also want to check in each time a blog publishes so you can send it out to all your social networking sites, like Facebook and Twitter. (More on this subject in chapter seven.) This task is very important and shouldn't be neglected. It represents one of the best ways to promote your blog and gain readers.

LINKING IN AND OUT

Everything you do that involves linking into or out of your blogged book helps SEO your blog. Google and other search engines like to see outgoing links to relevant and reputable websites just as much as they like to see links coming in to yours. This seems to indicate your blog's or website's degree of popularity or significance. So, as you write your blog posts, consider providing links to resources you find on the Internet. This helps your ranking on SERPs.

You'll also want to network with other bloggers who write about the same subject. See if they will agree to reciprocal linking. If so, offer to add them to your "blog roll," which is a widget, and then ask them to add you to theirs. A blog roll consists of a listing of links to your favorite blogs—or to blogs you feel will help your readers in some way. As such, it's a resource you provide your readers. It has historically been a superb way to increase your blogged book's SERPs. In 2008, however, Technorati.com decided to stop including links created by blog rolls in their ranking calculations. Thus these types of links are no longer quite so important. Search engines still see them as links, however, which keeps them relevant to SEO.

On my How to Blog a Book blog, my blog roll contains not only blogs about blogging and related subjects, but a few of my other blogs in case any readers are interested in seeing my other work. By linking back and forth between my own blogs, I increase their SEO and SERP to some extent.

If there's a blog out there that contains helpful information, or that you feel shouldn't be missed, but that blogger won't reciprocate with a link to your site, you can still list their link on your blog roll. It remains a helpful service to your readers.

Another way to add links to your blogged book involves commenting on other blogs. This entails going out and reading what other bloggers write on your topic and leaving comments. The comment box always offers you a way to provide a link back to your blogged book, usually by putting its website address in a response box along with your name and e-mail address. Additionally, this drives readers to your blogged book, which, in my mind, is as important as SERPs—or at least they go hand in hand.

In addition to linking in and out of your blogged book, consider linking within your own blog. (See "How to Compose Your Blog Posts" earlier in this chapter.) Creating a link that emphasizes the keywords of another blog post—yours or someone else's—is considered good form and a great strategy.

Any way you can link in and out of your blogged book will help your ranking and bring in readers. So, link, link, link.

RESPONDING TO BLOG COMMENTS

When you publish a post of particular interest to your readers, you know immediately—or almost immediately. Typically they let you know what they think about what you have written. This tends to be especially true if you write about something with which they strongly disagree or agree.

It's a good idea to reply to comments and to do so promptly. This lets your readers know that you appreciate them and the time they have taken not only to read your blog, but to tell you what they think of your posts. It also allows you to dialogue with them. In this way you encourage them to continue reading, to comment again in the future, and to tell their friends to read your blog as well.

Creating a dialogue with your blogged book readers constitutes an important blogging activity. If you can get your readers "talking," you can get valuable feedback on your book. That's what you want.

Many blog programs allow you to decide if anyone can post a comment or if you will moderate all comments. (As mentioned in chapter five, find this under the "Settings/Discussions" menu in WordPress.) There are also plug-ins, such as Akismet, that help get rid of spam comments. You should monitor the comments on your blogged book as well, which is another reason to stay on top of what's going on even if you are scheduling posts.

You reply to comments from within your blogging program's "Comment" menu. If you have chosen to moderate all comments, you can accept or deny comments. Once you have accepted a comment, you can go to the "Comment" menu and reply to it. At that point, you can ask commenters questions about your blog and its subject matter, and get more targeted feedback.

If you aren't getting comments, you might not have enough readers yet, be striking a chord with the readers you have, or be structuring your posts to invite comments. Sometimes readers are just shy. It takes a few people commenting before others speak up. At VibrantNation.com, readers comment often on my blog posts—the same ones I post at Write Nonfiction NOW! and As the Spirit Moves Me. I seldom get comments at Write Nonfiction NOW!, and I get just a few at As the Spirit Moves Me. I think there are more readers at VibrantNation.com and the culture or environment on that website breeds comments. At my other blog, My Son Can Dance, I get a lot of comments simply due to the nature of the blog and the readers. I've never gotten a huge number of comments at How to Blog a Book either.

HOW TO CREATE CONTENT THAT GETS RANKED HIGHLY BY SEARCH ENGINES

It matters little if you are blogging a book or simply blogging, content is king when it comes to getting traffic to your site. If you are trying to figure out how to create a blog with content that also gets noticed and moves you up in the SERPs, Google has some great advice. In fact, while Google uses certain algorithms to decide on search engine ranking, these are aimed at helping people find "high-quality" sites. That means they reduce the rankings of low-quality content and increase the rankings of high-quality content. Content remains king.

To help you produce high-quality content, why not use Google's standards? Doing so isn't so hard. No, you can't use its algorithms, but Google suggests you ask yourself the following questions, which are posted on its website. I suggest you ask those that apply to each and every post you publish as you write your blogged book.

- Would you trust the information presented in this article?
- Is this article written by an expert or enthusiast who knows the topic well, or is it more shallow in nature?
- Does the site have duplicate, overlapping, or redundant articles on the same or similar topics with slightly different keyword variations?
- Would you be comfortable giving your credit card information to this site?
- Does this article have spelling, stylistic, or factual errors?
- Are the topics driven by genuine interests of readers of the site, or does the site generate content by attempting to guess what might rank well in search engines?
- Does the article provide original content or information, original reporting, original research, or original analysis?
- Does the page provide substantial value when compared to other pages in search results?
- How much quality control is done on content?
- Does the article describe both sides of a story?
- Is the site a recognized authority on its topic?
- Is the content mass-produced by or outsourced to a large number of creators, or spread across a large network of sites, so that individual pages or sites don't get as much attention or care?
- Was the article edited well, or does it appear sloppy or hastily produced?
- For a health-related query, would you trust information from this site?

- Would you recognize this site as an authoritative source when mentioned by name?
- Does this article provide a complete or comprehensive description of the topic?
- Does this article contain insightful analysis or interesting information that is beyond obvious?
- Is this the sort of page you'd want to bookmark, share with a friend, or recommend?
- Does this article have an excessive amount of ads that distract from or interfere with the main content?
- Would you expect to see this article in a printed magazine, encyclopedia, or book?
- Are the articles short, unsubstantial, or otherwise lacking in helpful specifics?
- Are the pages produced with great care and attention to detail vs. less attention to detail?
- Would users complain when they see pages from this site?

If we are going to rely on Google to tell us how to get our blogged books noticed by search engines—which makes it easier for our blogged books to be found by readers—I'd like to also note that a time existed when a 150-word post was enough to be attractive to this search engine. Those days have passed. A post that gets noticed by Google now must have at least 250 words. No more writing lots of really short posts in an attempt to move up in the SERPs. You must have a more substantial amount of content in your blog or blogged books posts.

ARE BLOGS AND BLOGGED BOOKS PROTECTED BY COPYRIGHT LAWS?

I frequently get asked, "If someone blogs a book—actually composes it in the form of blog posts they publish on the Internet—do they need to worry about a copyright for that blogged book?" The question has been asked about blog copy in general as well.

I often offer a general answer: "As the blogger, when you hit the publish button, you copyright the material by becoming its publisher and publishing it."

More specifically, under the Copyright law of 1976, which went into effect in 1978, any work created in *any* fixed form is protected by copyright upon creation. That means that when a work is put into any fixed form—printed out from your home laser jet printer; published as an e-book, booklet, or POD book; or sent into cyberspace as a blog post, it is protected by copyright. Thus completed and published blog posts, or all the posts that make up a blogged book, comprise written works created in fixed form and are protected by copyright.

To be on the safe side, I consulted two attorneys who specialize in intellectual property, communications, and First Amendment law. They advised that writers and bloggers always print out their work. That means, as a precaution, simply create a hard copy of your blog posts before actually posting them on the Internet or print out your manuscript as you compose it.

Know that the so-called "Poor-man's Copyright," putting your work in an envelope and mailing it to yourself, only serves to prove *when* you wrote something not that *you* actually wrote it. In spite of not being terribly essential, it can be a handy piece of evidence should you need it.

You have a copyright the moment you reduce your original idea to a tangible—written—form, but without copyright registration you cannot sue for infringement. If you want to sue someone for infringement and collect damages, if you worry about being infringed, or if you ever want to bring a lawsuit against someone for infringement and collect money, having a document that says you own the copyright to your work certainly can be useful. It provides actual proof that you, indeed, are the copyright owner of that written work. To file for a copyright of your blogged book, go to http://www.copyright.gov/forms/. The fee to file a paper form is $65; the online fee is $35. I'd suggest, however, copyrighting the whole manuscript.

Actually filing your work with the copyright office can be time consuming and costly (since there is a fee) if you produce a lot of content. Doing so for daily blog posts seems out of the question. Since you are blogging a book, you can put the copyright notice on your actual blog somewhere noticeable if you like. In general, putting this symbol in its proper format on all your work sends the message that you claim ownership of your work. Additionally, if you ever need to sue for copyright infringement, it strengthens your case.

IT ALL COMES DOWN TO CONTENT

If you want to produce a blogged book people will read—one that generates traffic and gets the attention of a publisher sometime down the road (or simply gain you readers when you self-publish your book), you must produce good content and lots of it. No other way exists.

Sure you need to promote that blog. Yes, a topic about which people want to read and a unique angle on your topic help considerably, especially if your blog has a lot of competition. Plus, you need to post consistently, use keywords, write with passion and authenticity, and have a market. But when it's all said and done, great content draws readers. Period.

In a *Sioux City Journal* article posted on November 28, 2010, Tucker Max, a best-selling author and a blogger, said, "Content is 90 percent of any good blog. The 10 percent that's left? That's fixable. Anybody can learn good marketing or good design. But good content is most important."

Max's writing career started after law school, when he began detailing the events of his life—or, more specifically, his nightlife—to his friends via e-mail. "I had to write e-mails and I realized you can't bull---- your friends. You can't waste their time. So I had to write something that somebody else cares about. That's how I learned how to write."

Those e-mails led to a blog about a single guy's exploits with women, and then to the book *I Hope They Serve Beer In Hell*, which became a huge bestseller. Though a single guy's exploits with women may not seem like a great topic choice to some, all that mattered was that he posted good content on his blog on a regular basis, did it with passion and authenticity, and connected with people who wanted to read it. He met Google's, or some other search engine's criteria, and for these reasons his blog rose up the ranks. He developed platform (partly thanks to the fact that Miss Vermont sued him—the suit was covered by every major media network and newspaper—and MTV released a documentary on him). He got noticed. He got a book deal with Kensington Books in 2004. His second book, *Assholes Finish First*, came out in 2010, and he's got a movie deal. (As the saying goes, there's no such thing as bad publicity.)

Whatever your topic, you simply must turn out excellent content on a regular basis. Sit down and start blogging your book. Write one post at a time or many posts at a time. Create a manuscript. Create a book. Write it with all your heart and soul and all the passion you can muster. Let your readers know who you are, and they will come to read your blog. Next, let's help those readers find your blogged book.

CHAPTER 7:

DRIVING TRAFFIC (READERS) TO YOUR BLOG

Let's assume that you've written your first blog post. Maybe you composed an introduction to your book and published it in one or more posts. You may even have scheduled two more parts of the introduction to post later the same week. How are you going to drive traffic—readers—to your blog to read the beginning of your book? In other words, how will you publicize or promote your blog as you start blogging your book and as time goes on?

Remember back in chapter four when we worked on your blogged book's business plan and I said you needed to think about promotion? Now we begin putting that promotion plan into motion.

Do you have your business hat on?

MAKING SURE THE WORLD KNOWS YOU'VE PUBLISHED IN CYBERSPACE

The first step toward promoting your blogged book involves "claiming" your blog with blog catalogs or aggregators, such as Technorati.com or Blogcatalog.com. Technorati, which cataloged almost 1.3 million blogs in the fall of 2011, is by far the largest. Your blog should be one of them.

You can do the same at Blogcatalog, which works as an aggregator of more than one million blogs. Here someone could find and subscribe to your blog via RSS feed and have new posts waiting for them to read in their browser automatically. You can also track how many people have signed up for RSS feed.

Blogs' standing and influence in the blogosphere also are rated or ranked by these sites. It's a complicated system involving a variety of factors, and it changes as the blogosphere changes. In 2011, Technorati described how its ranking system, called "Authority," was used for calculations this way: "Authority is calculated based on a site's linking behavior, categorization, and other associated data over a short, finite period of time. A site's authority may rapidly rise and fall depending on what the blogosphere is discussing at the moment, and how often a site produces content being referenced by other sites." It adds that topical Authority measures a blog's influence within its subject category and that factors influencing this include linking behavior from blogs and posts in the same category, how well a blog's overall content matches the category in question, and other associated data. It's possible for a blog to have authority in several categories, and the authority in each category may be different.

Most agree that links back to your blogged book and how relevant these links are make the most difference to your Technorati Authority or ranking influence within its subject category. You may read the Technorati Authority FAQ page to get the whole idea and better understand what *Authority* means. When you list your blogged book on Technorati, be sure to check the listing and set your categories to the most relevant for your content.

You'll want to have your blog posts "pinged" to sites like Technorati and Blogcatalog automatically as well. Now that you've claimed your blogs so they can be found, let's look at this activity next.

PING! YOUR BLOG HAS BEEN PUBLISHED!

Every time you write a blog post and hit publish, you want to be sure that post is pinged. What is a ping? A ping is a push mechanism by which a blog notifies a server that its content has been updated. An XML-RPC signal, which is a set of specifications and implementations that allow software running on disparate operating systems and in different environments to make procedure calls over the Internet, is sent to one or more "ping servers." These then generate a list of blogs that have new content. That's a complicated way to say that when your blog post is pinged, a blog catalog or aggregator knows you have added new content. This ensures that people looking for blog posts or content on your subject matter on these sites can more easily find your blogged book.

In some cases, you have to manually ping your content or set up an account with these sites for this to happen. I used to manually ping my posts to Technorati when I used Blogger. In most cases, however, this service is automated if you set up your blog correctly, or if you sign up with a blog catalog or aggregator. In WordPress it's an automated service.

Setting up your blogged book to ping out your posts is pretty simple—at least in WordPress. After you log into your WordPress blog, go to "Settings," then "Writing," then scroll to the bottom where it says "Update Services." You'll see this: "When you publish a new post, WordPress automatically notifies the following site update services. For more about this, see Update Services on the Codex. Separate multiple service URLs with line breaks." Then you'll see a space to add site update services.

Here are services to add. I suggest you add at least the first one on this list. It's best to add them all:

http://rpc.pingomatic.com/
http://rpc.technorati.com/rpc/ping
http://blogsearch.google.com/ping/
    RPC2
http://1470.net/api/ping
http://api.feedster.com/ping
http://api.moreover.com/RPC2
http://api.moreover.com/ping
http://api.my.yahoo.com/RPC2
http://api.my.yahoo.com/rss/ping
http://bblog.com/ping.php

http://bitacoras.net/ping
http://blog.goo.ne.jp/XMLRPC
http://blogdb.jp/xmlrpc
http://blogmatcher.com/u.php
http://bulkfeeds.net/rpc
http://coreblog.org/ping/
http://mod-pubsub.org/kn_apps/
    blogchatt
http://www.lasermemory.com/lsrpc/
http://ping.amagle.com/
http://ping.bitacoras.com

http://ping.blo.gs/
http://ping.bloggers.jp/rpc/
http://ping.cocolog-nifty.com/xmlrpc
http://ping.blogmura.jp/rpc/
http://ping.exblog.jp/xmlrpc
http://ping.feedburner.com
http://ping.myblog.jp
http://ping.rootblog.com/rpc.php
http://ping.syndic8.com/xmlrpc.php
http://ping.weblogalot.com/rpc.php
http://ping.weblogs.se/
http://pingoat.com/goat/RPC2
http://rcs.datashed.net/RPC2/
http://rpc.blogbuzzmachine.com/
    RPC2
http://rpc.blogrolling.com/pinger/
http://rpc.icerocket.com:10080/
http://rpc.newsgator.com/
http://rpc.weblogs.com/RPC2
http://topicexchange.com/RPC2
http://trackback.bakeinu.jp/
    bakeping.php
http://www.a2b.cc/setloc/bp.a2b

http://www.bitacoles.net/ping.php
http://www.blogdigger.com/RPC2
http://www.blogoole.com/ping/
http://www.blogoon.net/ping/
http://www.blogpeople.net/servlet/
    weblogUpdates
http://www.blogroots.com/tb_
    populi.blog?id=1
http://www.blogshares.com/rpc.php
http://www.blogsnow.com/ping
http://www.blogstreet.com/xrbin/
    xmlrpc.cgi
http://www.mod-pubsub.org/
    kn_apps/blogchatter/ping.php
http://www.newsisfree.com/RPC-
    Cloud
http://www.newsisfree.com/
    xmlrpctest.php
http://www.popdex.com/addsite.php
http://www.snipsnap.org/RPC2
http://www.weblogues.com/RPC/
http://xmlrpc.blogg.de
http://xping.pubsub.com/ping/

Click on "Save Changes." Now watch your traffic increase.

AUTHORS MUST BECOME SAVVY SOCIAL NETWORKERS

In addition to pinging your posts each time you publish them, you'll want to use social networks to get the word out about what you've written. This means using Twitter, Facebook, and even LinkedIn to let your "tweeple," friends, followers, and connections know you've written something informative, useful, or entertaining. You also may want to begin using Google's new social networking site, Google+.

If you aren't already using social networking, start now. Do not wait. And don't dismiss social networking as a waste of time. It serves as one of the most important and effective ways to promote your book, build author platform and, ultimately, sell books. Also don't skimp; join all three of these networks. (And Google+, too.) If you aren't blogging about anything business related, you could get away without joining LinkedIn. However, consider your book a business and join anyway; then seek out like-minded people who might be interested in your book in the LinkedIn groups, which is where the real connecting happens on that site anyway. If you insist on being minimal, though, and don't think LinkedIn is for you, use Facebook and Twitter.

If you want to know how to use these networks, there are plenty of books to read and tons of information on the Internet you can access. Just search for "How to use Twitter" or "How to use Facebook," and you'll be up all night reading for a month. You can try:

- Dana Lynn Smith's series: *The Savvy Book Marketer's Facebook Guide for Authors*, *The Savvy Book Marketer's Twitter Guide for Authors* and *The Savvy Book Marketer's Guide to Successful Social Marketing* (http://SavvyBookMarketer.com)
- The resources offered by Joanna Penn at http://www.thecreativepenn.com/marketing
- Penny C. Sansevieri's *Red Hot Internet Publicity, An Insider's Guide to Marketing Your Book on the Internet* (Cosimo Books, June 2009)
- Jan Zimmerman and Doug Sahlin's *Social Media Marketing All-in-One For Dummies* (For Dummies, September 2010)
- Liana Evan's *Social Media Marketing: Strategies for Engaging in Facebook, Twitter and Other Social Media* (Que Publishing, June 2010)—or any book in this Que series on social media marketing
- The resources offered by socialmediaexaminer.com

- Mari Smith's *The New Relationship Marketing* and *Facebook Marketing: An Hour a Day*

I'm sure many of you don't want to learn to use social networks. Neither do the majority of my clients. "It's a waste of time," they tell me. "It means I have less time for my writing."

Well, it can be a waste of time and it can take a lot of time if you don't do your social networking effectively or economically. I'm here to say it can, indeed, be that time sink many writers fear it will become. I'm also here to say it does not have to be a time sink and to emphatically say again that social networking is a publicity *must* for any aspiring author. There are platforms to be built on social networks. You can build one there. Your blogged book is a start, but you must implement your publicity plan with social networking.

If you engage in social networking, this one activity will help you:

- CREATE A FAN BASE ON FACEBOOK, TWITTER, LINKEDIN, AND GOOGLE+. These people might later purchase your book. They also may circulate the information you post—the links to your blog posts, the date of your book release, the times and places where you are speaking or teaching. This allows their followers to read your status updates and click on your links, which, in turn, increases the chance that new people might check you out, read your blog, subscribe to your newsletter, follow you, purchase your book, etc.
- DEVELOP EXPERT STATUS. Every time you participate in forums and groups, such as those on Facebook or LinkedIn, or in any way post information about your topic, you demonstrate your expertise about your subject area and give other people in those groups, forums, and social networks a chance to notice this. They will look at your profile. They will click on the links you have provided and then possibly choose to subscribe to your blog, follow, or connect with you on a social network, or in some way become fans.
- INCREASE THE SEARCHABILITY OF YOUR NAME, YOUR BOOK, AND YOUR WEB SITE OR BLOG. Each time you join a social network you create a profile. This profile creates a link that can be found in search engines. This

profile also may have a place to link back to your website or blog. This increases traffic to your blogged book. The profile also mentions your name, your book, and your website. This makes all of these more findable in search engines because the social networks already rank highly in these search engines—more highly than your blogged book or website.

In these ways, social networking provides a superb way to build your platform.

TWEETING YOUR BLOGGED BOOK POSTS TO TWITTER

Twitter is a social network that focuses on 140-character messages that answer the question, "What are you doing?" Sometimes "tweeting," which is what you do when you post to Twitter, is called "microblogging" because it works much like blogging, only with a character limit. Once you post a tweet, other people can "retweet" it—send it along—to their "tweeple," or followers, thus creating a viral effect and exposing your update to many more people.

It's easy and free to use Twitter. Creating an account takes just a minute. Just complete your profile, upload a photo, and write a short bio. Link your account to your blog website.

Add the AddToAny: Share/Bookmark/Email Button, SexyBookmarks plug-in, or a similar social bookmarking plug-in, to your blog so your readers easily can tweet your posts on Twitter.

You also can add plug-ins that help you easily or automatically publish your blog posts to Twitter. You can try WP to Twitter, Twitter News Feed, or Post to Twitter, for instance.

If you have added only a social bookmarking plug-in to your blog and not one that automatically posts it to Twitter, each time you publish a post, you can "view this post" and use the share button that appears at the bottom of the post to tweet it (and share it on Twitter). These automatically shorten the URL and add the title of the post. You can add a message to go with the title if there are still characters left. (Remember you get only 140.) Or you can copy and paste the short link of your post into your Twitter status update along with a message. A short link is a short version of the long URL of your blog post. At the top of the page where you create a post, you will find a tab that says "Get Short Link." It appears after you have published your post. Click on it. The short link will pop up.

There is an etiquette to using Twitter. You'll want to Google this or utilize some of the resources I mentioned earlier in this chapter to learn how to follow other people and what type of information to post (I mentioned some earlier as well). There's a way to gain followers; I don't recommend the get-followers-fast schemes. Providing a lot of good information, getting involved in conversations, and following people back who seem interesting to you works best. As with blogging, good content works well. So keep blogging and linking to the posts, as well as linking to other great content.

As a writer and blogger, you will gain the most followers by:

- Staying on topic.
- Following other writers and bloggers.
- Following and actually conversing with other bloggers and writers interested in your topic.
- Retweeting the information of other writers and bloggers.
- Sharing information that is useful to other writers and bloggers.
- Letting people know about your progress.
- Supporting other writers and bloggers.
- Following and connecting with experts on your topic.
- Sharing content useful to experts on your topic.
- Tweeting at least three times a day, more if possible, and at different times of the day.

SHARING YOUR BLOGGED BOOK POSTS ON FACEBOOK

Facebook, another social network, is considered by some just a place to keep up with friends and family, but more and more people find it an extremely useful place to generate business. With this in mind, the savvy blogged book promoter wants to be sure to publish blog posts to Facebook regularly.

Once you have set up your free account by creating a profile, uploading a photo, and making sure you've included relevant links to your blogged book, you can begin manually uploading links to published posts if you like. You can do this in your status update bar where it asks you, "What's on your mind?" Simply say something like, "Did you know that sharing your posts on Facebook is really important for authors of blogged books?" You can then type in the Internet address of the link to your blog post (or even a shortened link), and Facebook will automatically add the post below your status update.

I must note that Facebook changes constantly; when I first wrote this section, Facebook had an icon about the status bar that said "link." You could click on it, and simply include the Internet address for your blog post. By the time I came back to do developmental edits on the manuscript, that icon was gone. Typing in the Internet address of your blog post in your status update seems consistently to work as a way to post a link.

You can make your blog posts automatically publish to Facebook by registering for "Networked Blogs." This is an "app" (application) that used to show up on the menu on the left side of the Facebook page under your photo, along with all the other apps and things, like BranchOut, Links, Photos, Hugs, etc. These days, the easiest way to find it is by typing "Networked Blogs" into Facebook's search engine.

Once you have the app, follow the instruction to register your blog. Also follow the directions to verify your blog.

Next go to your "Account Information" and click on the "Application" settings. Click on "edit settings" for Networked Blogs and be sure that under "Additional Permissions" you check the box there that allows posts to be published to your wall.

Now go to your Facebook home page and click on "Networked Blogs." Find your blog on the left and click on its name. You'll see your current blog posts on the left and a list on the right. Find "Feed Settings" and click on it. Under "Personal Profile," check the box that says "Auto-publish to personal profile." You can test this out to see if the most current posts appear on your wall. If you have any problems, be sure you went through the whole syndication process.

Below this, Facebook also offers a way to arrange to tweet your posts to Twitter and to Facebook pages as well. All that said, it's best to get involved on Facebook personally rather than in an automated manner. Again, Facebook changes its rules of operation frequently and experts like Mari Smith, author of *Facebook Marketing: An Hour a Day*, claim it's a better practice to take the time to publish updates with links to your blog posts manually even though it takes more time to do so. This ensures that a new change in Facebook practices does not affect you or your updates in any way.

OFFERING LINKS TO YOUR BLOGGED BOOK POSTS ON LINKEDIN

Publicizing your blog posts on LinkedIn poses a simple task. Once you have a free account—a much more detail-oriented task—you simply go to your profile page and under the "edit my profile" tab, click on "post an update." (This is a small option under the box with your name; it's off to the far right.) Before you hit the "share" button, you also can opt to check the Twitter settings button and have your update go to Twitter at the same time, thus managing two social networks with one click.

On LinkedIn you have the option of sharing links in your updates, so by all means, add the links to your recent blog posts. This is a great way to let people know you are blogging a book. If you are writing a book that has great information for professionals, LinkedIn is *the* place to share.

Your profile allows you one blog link; if you want to promote your blogged book and you have more than one blog, you better choose your blogged book. Be sure to customize it so the name of your blogged book appears. Also, you can have all your posts automatically show up in your public profile, not your status report, at LinkedIn by adding the WordPress application offered by LinkedIn. You can find this in the "More" category at the top of any LinkedIn page, at the very end of the menu bar running along the top of the page. Click on "More" and then scroll down to "WordPress." Fill out the form and you are good to go.

You also can start a group focused on your expertise in LinkedIn. This provides a powerful way to use this social network. In your own group, you can actually even syndicate your blog feed to post automatically on the discussion board. Members do not have this option. You can join groups and then post links to relevant blog posts in the discussion forum, but be sure to check the guidelines for the group before doing so.

HOW TO BECOME A SAVVY NETWORKER

If you do not want to end up spending all day and all night socializing on the Internet, you must become a savvy networker. You can use all sorts of products, such as TweetDeck.com, Hootsuite.com and Ping.fm, to help you consolidate your social networking activities. These programs help you do things like watch all your social networks at once, send one status update to all your networks with one click, and track the statistics on your status updates or links. They make your social networking more manageable. Join the networks and ask around to see what others use to help them keep their social networking streamlined. (Pay attention to status updates; sometimes these actually say what program the person used when he or she sent it.) Find out what the busiest social networkers are using to help them make their social networking time fast, easy, and efficient. If you ask them, they will be happy to tell you. Social networkers like to share; that's what it's all about, sharing great information.

What great information are you going to share? Your blogged book posts, and anything else that relates to your blogged book, or to you as an author, that might attract people to read your blogged book. For example, you can share:

- Related articles
- Other people's blog posts on the topic
- Your writing progress
- Related breaking news
- Related book reviews

- Related movies and documentaries
- Details of trips you take to research your blogged book
- Quotations
- Suggestions to go read your blogged book
- Information about your upcoming speaking engagements
- Tips related to your topic

The service I use most consistently to help me streamline my social networking and promote my blogs is HootSuite.com. With this one service I can actually take the link from one of my blogged book posts, shorten it, add it to a status update, and send this status update to three networks at once. I also can schedule this status update to go to all my social networks any time I like. So, if I've scheduled posts for a week, I can got to HootSuite.com and input all the links with a short message and then schedule them for the days the posts will publish. I can even send them to Twitter, for example, more than once in one day—early and late, since people use Twitter at different times and someone coming on late might have missed my earlier update.

I also can post and schedule all sorts of other messages to my social networks, such as those included in the list above. In this way, I automate my social networking.

If you want to track how many people follow your links after you've posted them, shorten them using bitly.com, and then put these links into HootSuite.com. Otherwise HootSuite.com will shorten them for you. You can also publish the links directly to your social networks from bitly.com. Bitly will then track how many people click on the link. Ping.fm is another service that will send out your posts. Hootsuite.com links to Ping.fm as well.

TweetDeck.com lets you keep track of all your "tweeple," friends, followers, and connections in an organized manner. You can see what's happening on all your social networks and if you've been mentioned or have received a direct message, etc., with HootSuite.com. I find the latter much simpler to use than Tweet-Deck.com, but many people love TweetDeck.com. You cannot, however, separate out your favorite people to follow like you can on TweetDeck.com.

Of course, you can post status reports with your blog post links or any other information from each social networking site separately, if these services sound too overwhelming. As I mentioned earlier, I suggest doing this on Facebook anyway, since the rules of engagement change there so quickly.

MARKING BLOGGED BOOK PAGES WITH SOCIAL BOOKMARKING

A short note on marking your posts with social bookmarking will bring you up to speed on this subject. Social bookmarking involves using services like StumbleUpon.com, Digg.com, reddit.com, and Delicious.com. These sites suggest content based on users' preferences and reading or search history.

Here's how it works: After you write a post, you share the link on one of these services. Doing so requires that you set up an account. There are some who say using this type of social bookmarking can get your post indexed by Google faster than many other methods, even e-zine article marketing, which is known for extremely fast indexing. (More information on that later in this chapter). However, others say social bookmarking only works well when you have a group of people who work together to add each other's blog posts and rate them. You can try it both ways—on your own and with a group of blogging friends willing to help with the social bookmarking task.

Or you can simply hope your readers go to the trouble of adding your posts to these sites. You can also ask them to do so.

USING VIDEO TO DRIVE TRAFFIC TO YOUR BLOGGED BOOK

Another increasingly popular way to drive traffic to blogs involves video. In May 2010, YouTube announced that it had exceeded two billion video views per day. Seven months later, YouTube announced that its users had uploaded more than

13 million hours of video content to its servers in the last twelve months, resulting in more than 700 billion YouTube video views. YouTube videos have become an ever-more popular form of Internet information and entertainment, and it's one bloggers and book bloggers can and should use to drive traffic to their sites.

Since YouTube constitutes one of the most popular websites on the Internet today, you want to have a presence there. If you have a YouTube channel, you can post videos related to your blog to YouTube. You can share this link via your social networks and, if you've included a link to your blog somewhere in the video description, viewers can find your blogged book. Also, by posting these videos in your blogged book posts, you can drive enormous amounts of traffic to your blogged book. (All blogging software has a function whereby you can add video right into your blog posts.)

Most computers, especially laptops, these days have video capability, and "flip" digital video cameras are pretty inexpensive and easy to use. Without going into a ton of detail, let me just say that once you have figured out how to videotape yourself, you can upload that video to YouTube. The videos do not have to be perfect. In fact, sometimes it's the most imperfect videos that get the most views or go viral.

Here's what you do: Create an account on YouTube. Then sign in. Upload what you have already recorded either on your computer or with your webcam. If you don't like the quality of your videos, reshoot using different lighting or a microphone.

What do you record? Any of the following:

- A blog post
- Information about your blog
- Your mission statement
- The benefits of reading your blogged book
- Tips or tools from your blogged book
- A book trailer
- A report on your writing or blogging process

Be creative and have fun. Record whatever you think might be fun for you to talk about or interesting for viewers to watch and hear. Who knows, maybe your video will go viral. And by all means, share it wherever you can … on all your social networks! At the least you might have a lot of your friends on Facebook or "tweeple" on Twitter share your video!

USING E-ZINE ARTICLE MARKETING TO DRIVE TRAFFIC TO YOUR BLOGGED BOOK

While I encourage you to publish articles related to your blogged book in traditional print publications—magazines and newspapers certainly carry a lot of clout—when it comes to driving traffic to your blogged book, one of the easiest and most effective ways to start building your platform involves writing and publishing articles for online publications. Many print publications have online versions that offer different content, but e-zines, newsletters, and magazines that publish only on the Internet often look for free content to fill their pages. Other bloggers, too, look for guest posts or free content to fill their blogs.

It's easy enough to do a Google or Yahoo search for e-zines and blogs on the subject of your blogged book, and then to submit articles to those you find. You can even submit excerpts from your chapters—blog posts grouped together to form an article; this provides you with a source of articles you don't have to write from scratch, and the editor or blogger might even allow you to say they are excerpts, which would promote your book further. Targeted e-zines and blogs provide your best promotional article tool online, since they have a built-in audience interested in your subject.

You usually can submit articles to e-zines for free; however, doing so can be quite time consuming if you have a large number of articles. Therefore, in addition to submitting to specific e-zines that hit your target market, it behooves you to find an article directory to which you can submit your work as well. Directories provide free content to hundreds of different e-zines and bloggers looking for articles to fill their pages. In addition, anyone who chooses to publish your article is required to include a "resource box" with your bio and information that directs readers to your website or blog or that mentions your blogged book.

The easiest and least time consuming method for getting your articles in the most e-zines involves paying for an article distribution service. For a nominal fee, these companies allow you to submit your article and then turn around and submit that article to other article directories and e-zines for you. In this manner, your articles or news releases get the most exposure and may end up in any number of e-zines. Actually, it's quite amazing where articles land when you let the editors of all types of e-zines and authors of all sorts of blogs pick and choose content from these directories. If you don't want to pay for this service, you can simply submit to a few e-zine directories and to certain blogs on your own.

There are numerous e-zine directories online. You can do a search for them and easily begin submitting articles. Most offer a free service to writers. Here are a few popular ones (if you only submit to one, choose EzineArticles.com, the largest.):

- EzineArticles.com
- ArticlesFactory.com
- Articles.EveryQuery.com
- Amazines.com
- ArticlesBase.com
- ArticleBiz.com
- ArticleCity.com
- IdeaMarketers.com
- ArticleRamp.com
- ArticleDepot.co.uk

Here are a few article submission and distribution services you might try:

- SubmitYourArticle.com
- isnare.com
- ArticleMarketer.com
- ThePhantomWriters.com

Each service has its own guidelines on article length, resource boxes, bios, and such, and none of them pay you for your content.

Always use the resource box well. Direct readers of your article back to your blogged book. List your blogged book's website address in the resource box.

One note of caution: Google has been cracking down on something called "duplicate content," and this caused some concern in the world of e-zine article marketing. When Google spots duplicate content on a blog or website, it can actually lower its ranking. To avoid this problem, the best rule of thumb is to make sure the article or blog post on your website or blog contains 20 percent different content from the article you post in a directory or vice versa. Also, to avoid any problems with the e-zine directories or distributors, be sure you always write under the same name and have a similar bio. You can change your e-zine articles using "spinning" software that's available on the Internet; some distributors offer a spinning service as well. Spinning is the act of changing titles, words, and sentences in your article to create several versions of the same piece. Also, add this WordPress plugin to your blog: PubSubHubbub. It puts a time stamp on each post to show Google when your post was published. This distinguishes your blog post from your e-zine articles to some extent.

INCREASING TRAFFIC BY COMMENTING ON BLOGS

Another way to publicize your blogged book or blog involves commenting on other bloggers' posts. You know how you love it when readers leave comments on your blog posts, and how excited you got the first time a reader actually left a comment? Now it's time to do the same for other bloggers. Let me explain why.

Each time you comment on someone else's blog, you create a link back to your blogged book—that is, if you leave your blogged book's Web address behind.

Don't ever opt for an anonymous comment. Always choose to have your website or blog address used in conjunction with your name. Then when your name appears with your comment, readers can click on it and the link will take them directly to your blog.

Not only do all these links increase traffic to your blogged book, they also increase your Google ranking. The more often you leave comments, the more chances you have of getting blog readers from other popular blogs to check out what you are writing. The more people who check out your blog, the higher your blog goes in the SERPs. And the higher up it goes in the SERPs, the more easily it is found.

So go out and read blogs that have content that's related to your blog. These are the blogs you identified as complementary or competing blogs in chapter four. And be sure to leave a comment.

If you found books that were competing or complementary books, see if the authors of those books have blogs. Read their posts consistently and leave comments.

Do not spam these bloggers, however. By this, I mean don't simply leave links to your blog in the comment box. You must say something worthwhile; leave behind some useful information. Tell the blogger what great information he has provided, and then piggyback on his information with superb information of your own. The link to your blogged book will appear automatically if you opt to have your name link back to your blogged book.

I know that reading other blogs and commenting on them can be a time-consuming activity, and you'd rather be writing your blogged book. One way to handle this in a time-effective manner involves Google Alerts. Type "Google Alerts" into the Google search engine and click on "create an alert." Fill out the form with whatever search terms apply to your blog. Then whenever someone writes about your topic, you will be alerted and can click through the link to read the article or post. You can also subscribe to the blogs you find most relevant to your subject.

YOU NEED CONTENT ... SO GET WRITING!

The key to all of social networking and promoting online comes down to the same point I made at the end of the last chapter: Content is king. That means, the ultimate way to drive people to your blog (or website) is to produce great copy consistently and often—and to share it. The more superb and useful your content, the more readers and traffic you will get to your blog or website. This also helps you rise in the SERPs. So it's time to get writing!

I see more and more bloggers offering great, free content on their blogs and social networking sites every day. The amount of content they produce amazes me. They could be writing books, and maybe they are. In any case, the content they produce offers added value to any and all who read their words. I for one know I often find myself clicking through to discover who these people are and what else they are writing.

With that in mind, I encourage you to offer great content that attracts readers (and agents and publishers). Offer it in your blogged book, in your social networking updates, in your e-zine articles, and in the comments you leave at other blog sites. Also offer free guest posts to other bloggers. However, while I feel strongly that content, indeed, is king, I would have to admit that many other things must be done to differentiate your writing from the other writers and bloggers out there—and every day more bloggers decide to enter the cyber publishing world.

How will you differentiate yourself amongst the million voices all striving to get the same attention and readership? How will you reach out to an audience already drowning in noise? Melissa Tamura from Zen College Life at SmartBloggerz.com asked that question. She answered it by saying, "Good content alone will not do the trick—there has to be something more than just hoping that people will read your blog entries." I've covered many of those ways in this book already. But keep that in mind as you write.

PROMOTING YOUR BLOGGED BOOK OFF LINE

Don't forget about those off-line promotion activities I mentioned in chapter four when you were creating your business plan, such as public speaking, media appearances, newsletters, print media, and such. These offer great opportunities to drive traffic to your blogged book. They may seem counterintuitive, but they're actually not. You can garner blogged book readers in a variety of traditional places.

I suggest you do lots of public speaking. While many authors and writers balk at speaking, this remains the tried-and-true way to build platform and gain readers. Plus, you can send around a clipboard at each event with a sign-up sheet for your mailing list. Doing so gives you a chance to remind these new fans that you do, indeed, have a blogged book they can read. You can offer them an incentive for subscribing to your blog and to your newsletter, such as a free gift of some sort.

Go to networking events and pass out your business card. Make sure the blog address is on the card. Introduce yourself as the author of your blogged book. This is a great conversation starter. Encourage your new connections to go read your blogged book.

Send out press releases to the media. Let them know about your blogged book. Tie your subject into the news whenever possible. This provides a surefire way to get media attention. Radio and television interviews always lead to new readers (or book sales).

Subscribe to HARO at HelpAReporter.com, to Steve Harrison's Reporter Connection (ReporterConnection.com), or Drew Gerber's PitchRate.com, free services that let you know when reporters need expert sources for interviews. Then check these listings each time they arrive in your e-mail box and respond to those queries that apply to you, your expertise, and your blogged book or its subject matter.

Write articles related to your topic and send them out to journals and magazines. It's true less print media outlets exist today than in the past, but you may find some willing to publish an article or essay related to your blogged book. Don't worry about getting paid. Ask to have a byline and the link to your blog published instead.

Use traditional book marketing and promotion tools. You can find many of them in the following books:

- *1,001 Ways to Promote Your Book* by John Kremer (Open Horizons, May 2006)
- *Guerrilla Marketing for Writers* by Mike Larsen, Jay Conrad Levinson, and Rick Frishman (Morgan James Publishing, January 2010)
- *Guerrilla Publicity: Hundreds of Sure-Fire Tactics to Get Maximum Sales for Minimum Dollars Includes Podcasts, Blogs, and Media Training for the Digital Age* by Jay Conrad Levinson, Rick Frishman, and Jill Lublin (Adams Media, September 2008)

- *The Frugal Book Promoter: How To Do What Your Publisher Won't* by Carolyn Howard-Johnson (Star Publish, July 2004)
- *Grassroots Marketing for Authors and Publishers* by Shel Horowitz (Accurate Writing & More, March 2009)

Put on your thinking cap. Think outside the box, again. Find ways to promote your blogged book everywhere possible online and off. Don't miss an opportunity to tell someone about your book. Use that pitch you created in chapter four every chance you get. If you do this, you will find the number of unique readers to your blogged book growing daily. And what could be better than that? Maybe finishing your blogged book and getting a book deal!

CHAPTER 8:

I'VE FINISHED MY BLOGGED BOOK, NOW WHAT?

As you approach the end of your blogged book manuscript and get ready to publish the last post, consider your next step. Hopefully, this decision has been handled for you along the way. While you were still blogging your book, you received a call or an e-mail from an agent or an acquisitions editor who discovered your blogged book because of its popularity on the Internet and simply loved what you have written to date. The traffic you drove to your blogged book on a daily basis due to your promotional efforts provided necessary proof that a market exists for a printed book on your topic. If an agent contacted you, she asked for a proposal, which you had ready and waiting, offered to represent you and, subsequently, landed you a traditional publishing deal. If an acquisitions editor from a publishing house called, he asked for a proposal, and then offered you a contract. In either case, you succeeded in accomplishing your goal. You wrote your book, published it, promoted it, and built enough platform at the same time to get discovered and published traditionally. You have both a blogged book and a traditionally printed book to show for it. Whoo-hoo!

DEAR AGENT OR EDITOR, DID YOU HAPPEN TO NOTICE MY BLOGGED BOOK?

What if your book has not been discovered by an agent or publisher as you blogged it, and it's now time to hit "publish" on that final post? Don't hang your head and assume you failed. You might feel disappointed, but your efforts have not been for naught. You have produced the first draft of a manuscript, which exists on the Internet. Anyone interested can sample your superb writing, and well-honed and carried-out concept.

Plus, you have built some amount of platform. If you have done all the things discussed in this book thus far, you should have unique readers and page views to show for your efforts. (If you don't, you need to increase your promotional efforts.) You can feel proud of that as well—and you can and should talk about these facts to acquisitions editors and to literary agents.

If you're a traditional publishing holdout—an aspiring author who really does not want to self-publish a printed version of her blogged book—and this blogged book "exercise" managed to get you to write your whole manuscript but didn't get you discovered, you have three things left to do: Write a fabulous query, write a phenomenal proposal, and approach a literary agent or a small or midsized publisher.

Literary agents work as writers' business partners. They represent you to publishing houses, or more accurately, to publishing houses' acquisitions editors (the ones responsible for finding new books to publish). They also look out for your best interests when it comes to negotiating the publishing contract. A superb agent also will have your long-term career goals in mind. To find agents and discover what kind of submissions they would like to receive, look in the annual edition of Writer's Digest's *Guide to Literary Agents, Writer's Market* or *Jeff Herman's Guide to Book Publishers, Editors, & Literary Agents.*

Small and midsized publishers will accept unagented work, meaning a proposal and ultimately a manuscript, presented by authors not represented by literary agents, but large publishers (and some midsized publishers) will not. Some agencies also have websites with guidelines offered online. You can approach the small and midsized publishers on your own if you like; some agents will approach these for you, but many will not.

Here's the great news: You have already done the groundwork—created a business plan—that allows you to quickly begin submitting a book proposal to agents and publishers. If a traditional publishing deal remains your dream, begin writing a query letter and a book proposal immediately (if you don't already have one). In fact, if you are reading this long before that last blog post goes out into cyberspace, start composing these documents and sending them out now. Be proactive. No need to wait to be found. Help those agents and publishers along. You can send out your query letter at any point after you start blogging your book.

If you haven't yet written your proposal, go back to chapter four and take all the information you compiled during the proposal process and put a proposal together. The proposal contains not just the nine essential elements we used in the proposal process, but also the complete list of sixteen a publisher uses to determine whether your book fits their list of published books (and those they plan to publish in the future). The publisher will also gauge whether a market exists for the book and if he feels you are both the right person to write the book and the best person to become the company's business partner. Remember, the sixteen parts of a proposal are:

- Introduction
    - Overview
    - Markets
    - Subsidiary Rights
    - Spin-Offs
    - Promotion
    - Competing Titles
    - Complementary Titles
    - Resources Needed to Complete the Book
    - About the Author
    - Mission Statement
    - Author's Platform

- Outline
  - List of Chapters
  - Chapter Summaries
  - Sample Chapters

If you aren't sure what a proposal looks like or what format one should have, there are some great books on the market, like Michael Larsen's *How to Write a Book Proposal,* Jeff Herman and Deborah Levine Herman's *Write the Perfect Book Proposal*, and Sheree Bykofsky and Jennifer Basye Sander's *The Compete Idiot's Guide to Getting Published*. (I have a workbook, *How to Evaluate Your Book for Success,* that takes writers through the proposal process and helps them accumulate the information necessary for a proposal. I also have a product called *The Easy-Schmeazy Nonfiction Book Proposal Template* that helps aspiring authors drop material into a proposal format. Both of these products are available at http://copywrightcommmunications.com/products.) Other books and products can be found on the Internet as well.

Put your book proposal together and have it professionally edited. The nonfiction book proposal represents the most important selling document you will create. As the old adage goes, "You only have one chance to make a first impression." That holds true when pitching a book. Let a professional editor help you make the best first impression possible. Make every word count, and present an error-free document. Also, be sure the editor you choose knows what goes into a nonfiction book proposal; many do not. Don't use just any editor. You can find editors on LinkedIn, at writers' conferences, in writers' clubs, through referrals from other authors, or even from agent referrals (ask their assistants).

Then write a great query letter and have this edited professionally as well. A query letter contains three things: a lead paragraph that entices an agent or publisher to want to read your manuscript, your pitch plus information about the length of your book and its benefits to readers or the special features you want to highlight, and why you are the perfect person to write the book. If you want to learn more about how to write a query letter, check out *How to Write Irresistible Query Letters* by Lisa Collier Cool, *Making the Perfect Pitch: How to Catch a Literary Agent's Eye* by Katharine Sands, *The Writer's Digest Guide to Query Letters* by Wendy Burt-Thomas, or *How to Write Attention-Grabbing Query & Cover Letters* by John Wood.

Once the letter is honed and flawless, send it to the agents you would like to have represent you, or to the small or midsized publishers your feel are right for your book. Typically, the proposal does not go out with the query letter, although some agents or publishers may ask to see it along with a query letter. Again, check guidelines in *The Guide to Literary Agents, Writer's Market,* or *Jeff Herman's Guide to Book Publishers, Editors, & Literary Agents* or the websites for each specific agent or publisher.

If your query gets a positive response, you will send off your proposal as requested along with a cover letter. Then you'll wait for a response. If you get a rejection, repeat the process. You can send more than one query, or a simultaneous submission, if you prefer. Sometimes, however, it's best to wait and see what response you get to your query and proposal so you can make adjustments to your proposal based upon the feedback you receive—that is, of course, if you don't get an acceptance immediately. Some agents and publishers prefer not to receive multiple submissions.

Don't give up if you are rejected many times. Even the best authors received hundreds of rejection letters. I've heard this advice: When you get a rejection letter, just say, "Next." Or say, "I must have sent that query to the wrong address. Next time I'll send it to the right address."

FROM BLOGGER TO SELF-PUBLISHER

If you don't want to pursue a traditional publishing deal (or don't land one), consider alternative ways of getting your manuscript off the Internet and into some sort of print version. As a blogger, you already have been self-publishing your book on the Internet. However, you can step up your game a notch or two and begin self-publishing print books as well.

You might, for instance, take your manuscript and produce a print-on-demand (POD) book. This is not so difficult to do and a fairly inexpensive option.

With this type of self-published book, you can print as few as twenty books in many cases or none at all. As buyers purchase books, more copies are printed "on demand"—one at a time. Another option is offset printing, the "true self-publishing" route, which typically requires printing large quantities of books you might need to store in your garage.

Or you can take a more high-tech approach and turn your blogged book into an e-book. Today, this constitutes a great option if you don't want to spend a lot of money and want your book available for the variety of e-readers on the market today. As e-book sales surpass print book sales, authors who don't make their books available on e-readers miss a great sales opportunity. Plus, this is the most inexpensive self-publishing option and allows you to get in on today's biggest publishing trend.

Of course, you can just leave your blogged book up as a completed blogged book. However, if it remains dormant for long, it will lose readership. People still will find it as they use search engines for particular terms and phrases, but it will fall in the SERPs if you don't add new content. If you choose this option, consider adding a new post once a week at a minimum.

If you leave the blog dormant as a sales page for a printed book or e-book as well, simply add copy occasionally to help drive buyers to the site. Again, it's better to keep adding content (i.e., keep the blog alive) and drive traffic there to increase book sales.

TURNING YOUR BLOGGED BOOK INTO A POD BOOK

If you want to self-publish your blogged book as a printed book, you can choose several methods to do so. First, however, you must have a manuscript.

As I mentioned previously, the easiest way to blog a book and end up with a manuscript entails writing your posts in Microsoft Word (or a similar program) and then copying and pasting them into your blogging software. If you have done this, you now have a complete manuscript. If you haven't done this, you will need to copy and paste all your blog posts into a document—quite a chore.

Even if you have created a manuscript, you will want to go back to your blog and look for information to add to your manuscript from reader comments and your replies. Also, if you planned to add fresh copy or features to your printed book, this is the time to do so, before you hand the manuscript over to your editor or book designer.

Once you have a manuscript comprised of all your posts, divide your posts into chapters—if you didn't do this earlier. Then edit the chapters to make sure the posts flow together smoothly and read well. You don't want them to be choppy or to sound like a bunch of 250-word posts. At this point, these short posts need to sound like sections in a longer chapter. Your post titles should read like subheads. Edit out all references to previous posts or to what posts are coming next. Unless you are creating an e-book, take out all links or fully write them out. (If you are creating an e-book, you will want to include links.) Make sure you delete all references to "this blog" or "this blogged book" from your manuscript. It should now make reference to a "book" instead, since readers will read a printed book not a blogged book. Check that you don't have too many lists or questions with answers as well.

Once you have edited the manuscript, send it to a professional editor for another round of polishing (or two or three). Do not skip this step or skimp here. Many self-published authors fail to have their manuscripts professionally edited and end up with books that do not meet the same quality standards of traditionally published books. Don't let your book fall into this category after all your hard work. It will not sell well if it is obviously self-published, and this fact will be evident in its lack of professional editing.

You want both developmental and copyediting or line editing. You may also want content editing. Developmental editors will check that everything in your book makes sense, flows, and that nothing is missing or misplaced. They may delete or move copy. They will point out redundancies, inconsistencies, and make suggestions on how you can improve your book. Content editors check your content to make sure it is correct: that the period clothing you describe is accurate, that the facts you mention are correct, that the dates that parallel news events related to your story line up. Copy or line editors correct grammar, punctuation, and syntax and generally strengthen your sentence structure and overall writing. It's usually best to hire a developmental editor for the first round of editing and then a copy or line editor for the second round of editing; sometimes an editor will do both types of editing. The best editing jobs involve two or three rounds of editing, sometimes more. You could have two rounds with a developmental editor to make sure you strengthen your book in general, and then two rounds of line editing to ensure your writing ends up clean and strong. You could throw in a round of content editing as well.

Even great writers need a great editors. Most writers are too close to their work to edit well themselves. Your book and you will appear unprofessional if the manuscript contains errors.

You also should consider hiring an indexer; most nonfiction books benefit from an index and it's best completed by a professional. You also may want to have someone create a glossary for your book. Don't let your book fail because you skimped on these things either.

Last, but not least, hire a proofreader. Proofreaders provide a different skill than editors do. They catch all the minor errors made during editing—a word not caught by the spell-checker, a second period left unnoticed amongst the many changes made, too many spaces between words, possibly even a stray comma that doesn't fit the style used throughout the book.

At this point, you need to convert the manuscript into a book design format. Simpler said than done—especially for writers. Do not design the book yourself unless you have professional design skills. Another distinction between many self-published books and their traditionally published counterparts can be found in design. Don't raise the self-published flag with unprofessional design. Instead, hire a professional book designer.

Covers sell books, so be sure your book cover looks professional. You can purchase cover photos with subscriptions to such services as iStockphoto.com. Your book designer should know all about photo and art permissions and how to make stock photos look unique to your cover. Many POD publishers, usually subsidy or author services publishers like BookLocker, iUniverse, Xlibris, PublishAmerica, and Lulu, offer packages that include cover and interior design. The more unique your cover and interior, the better. A professional designer who does not work for one of these subsidy publishers will give you a design unlike anyone else's.

You can produce a POD book using a subsidy or author services press, which offer a variety of services to help you, like editing and design. Their editing services will likely be light copy or line editing; sometimes they provide developmental editing. If you use their design services you may end up with a design not as unique as you'd like. Plus, with their template cover designs, you run the risk of other books having the exact same cover image or one that's similar to yours. Most will publish your book under their imprint as well. This means the subsidy press's name will appear on the bound side, or spine, of the book because they provide the ISBN. This also means you are not the publisher of record; they are. This is fine if:

- You don't plan on becoming your own publishing house and running a business as a book publisher—the true meaning of self-publishing.
- You want help and hand holding every step of the way through the self-publishing process.
- You don't want to learn how to self-publish (you just want to get your book published).
- You don't want to hire editors, a designer, purchase an ISBN, etc.

It's not fine, if:

- You plan on self-publishing more than one book.
- You want to create a publishing company.
- You want to have all your books published under your imprint—your publishing company name—and have that name on the spine of the book.
- You want to learn how to do everything necessary to self-publish a book or hire people to help you.
- You don't mind hiring and managing editors and a designer, purchasing ISBNs, etc.

If you fall into the latter category, you can contract these services on your own and then go directly to a POD printer, like Lightning Source or even Amazon's CreateSpace, and have the book printed. (BookLocker allows you to use your own ISBN as well.) If you do the latter, you can decide on your own publishing company name and print your book under this imprint. Then this name will be printed on the book's spine and you become the publisher of record. Now you have truly self-published your book.

OTHER BLOG-TO-PRINT-BOOK OPTIONS

If you want to become a full-fledged self-publisher, you can go to an offset printer. These printers specialize in short-run book manufacturing, and they are by far the most economical option for printing (the best quality, too). In this case, you have to actually order copies of your book, store them, and ship them out yourself (unless you opt for a distributor).

If you don't want to print one thousand books, or you need books quickly, there are printers who use other types of presses and will print short runs extremely fast; the price per book is higher but still affordable. You will have to ship the books to buyers or opt for a distributor. In some cases, they will distribute to Amazon.

There are many great books out there about how to self-publish, such as Dan Poynter's *Self-Publishing Manual*, *The Complete Guide to Self-Publishing* by Marilyn Ross and Sue Collier, *The Indie Author Guide* by April L. Hamilton, *Self-Publishing For Dummies* by Jason R. Rich, and *The Fine Print of Self-Publishing, Fourth Edition—Everything You Need to Know About the Costs, Contracts, and Process of Self-Publishing* by Mark Levine. Be sure to consult these great resources for all the things you need to produce and print your blogged book.

You might also want to check out companies that convert your blog to a book without changing a thing, such as Blurb.com, Bookemon.com, and Blog-2Print.SharedBook.com. This is a great option if you want your printed book to appear identical to your blogged book, though I don't recommend this for a book that you want to read like an actual book. If for some reason, however, that's what you want, simply do a search on any search engine and you will find a variety of companies that offer blog-to-book services. Also research what options they offer, if any, when it comes to design or editing. I recommend FastPencil.com. Their program offers the ability to reformat using their design templates once your blog has been imported. FastPencil also offers typical POD services, such as distribution and subsidy press services, such as editing and cover design.

Once you have that printed book in hand, start selling it! Go back to what you've already learned about promotion.

TURNING YOUR BLOGGED BOOK INTO AN E-BOOK

If you don't want to incur much expense, you can simply convert your blogged book into an e-book and become an e-book publisher. In this way, you can enter the newest and fastest growing area of the publishing industry, one that is quickly surpassing printed books. If you choose to take this route, you can sell your e-book from your blogged book site or from a website, as well as from Amazon.com and Smashwords.com, thus making it readily available for all e-readers.

It used to be that authors created e-books simply by making PDFs of Microsoft Word documents. You can still do this and make your content available to your readers. Creating this type of e-book is pretty simple, but you do need some design savvy. If you plan to charge a fair amount, you must create an e-book that looks nice and has some decent graphics. After that, you need only get yourself a copy of Adobe Acrobat Professional or download a free PDF program. Save your finished manuscript as a secure PDF, and you are ready to sell it. (If you don't have any design ability, you can save your Word document, but it may not look pretty.)

Many people ask if this PDF needs to be password protected, which means you must give the person who buys the e-book a password to open the document. This is supposed to curtail illicit sharing of the e-book. You can password protect it if you like. I've never yet purchased one that was. Most people treat these PDF e-books—and all e-books—just like printed books, which are purchased and then lent out if they are well liked. Basically you want them to be shared. You want them to go viral, if possible.

There are some terrifically easy ways to create e-books for all e-reader formats that cost almost nothing these days. For instance, you can take your Word document and upload it to an e-book distributor and publisher, like Smashwords.com. If the formatting is correct, it will pass their conversion requirements and then become available in almost every e-reader format. (At the time of this printing, Smashwords had not yet set up an agreement with Amazon's Kindle.) You may, however, want to hire someone to make sure your Word document meets Smashword's requirements; this conversion can cost as little as $50 and a list of vendors who do this is available at the site. Additionally a style guide is available at Smashwords, and most people can follow it and create a document that passes Smashword's requirements. When I uploaded my first e-book, I followed the style guide and then asked someone on the list to check my work. I paid a minimal amount because I had done most of what was necessary (and learned a lot in the process). She tweaked a few things and my document passed with flying colors.

Additionally you will need a front cover design for your e-book. Any book designer can do this for you, or you can hire an e-book designer. E-book cover designers tend to be cheaper. I had a cover done for $50 for one of my e-books. Once they provide you with the high-resolution artwork, you upload it to Smashwords. It appears as a thumbnail in the Smashwords catalog. You need a designer who is aware of this fact.

After your book has been loaded at Smashwords and approved, Smashwords begins distributing it for you and you begin selling books. For this service, they take a minimal percentage of the book's selling price.

You can find a similar service at FastPencil.com; however, it does not sell to quite as many e-reader devices and the conversion process has a fee attached. Other e-book publishers and distributors exist as well, like BookBaby.com. Check out their fees, royalty schedules, and distribution range.

If you choose to produce a POD book at Amazon, for a small fee they will convert your book to an e-book as well. This is really a great deal.

I suggest combining the Smashwords.com service with the Amazon Kindle service to make sure your e-book is available to everyone. Take your document and your artwork and upload it to Amazon's Kindle. The same person who did your conversion for Smashwords can prepare it for the Kindle. Your cover designer can produce a cover that works for both sites. Then advertise on your blogged book's site that the e-book is available at both sale locations.

If all these options for turning your blogged book into something more tangible haven't set your mind reeling, here's something else to think about: Creating a printed or e-book really just comes down to recycling, or repurposing, your writing into another form—one that brings in income. Books, however, represent only one way to do that. Are you ready to explore other means of putting all that content you created to use? Then move on to the next chapter.

CHAPTER 9:

HOW TO REPURPOSE YOUR BLOG POSTS FOR PROFIT AND PROMOTION

Here's a little bit of information the book industry doesn't like to reveal: Books don't provide a huge source of income. In fact, most authors, with the exception of those who consistently hit the best-seller lists, supplement their book royalties with additional sources of income that may or may not be related to their publishing efforts. As an author and a blogger who has just produced or may be in the process of producing amazing amounts of content, you have a great advantage. You can turn all that content into money-making products. You can develop "information products" that create multiple streams of income and a business that revolves around your book. Many nonfiction books lend themselves to this.

While many of you reading this book picked it up so you could, indeed, begin blogging your book from start to finish and get discovered along the way, some of you may have stumbled upon it after you already began blogging. Maybe you'd been blogging for a while and achieved some success, which led you to wonder, "Maybe

I could turn my blog into a book." Or maybe you thought about some of those blog-to-book success stories, like *Julie & Julia* or *Stuff White People Like*, and thought, "That could be me. I could get discovered, too." Or maybe you began blogging a book after you had already created a successful blog on another topic.

If you didn't blog a book but you have an existing blog, you might have a lot—a whole lot—of blog content you could put to use that may not fit into just one book. Now you need to figure out how to recycle, or repurpose, all that content for profit as well as for promotion.

You see, each time you create an information product, not only can you sell it, you also can advertise it on your blog and through all your social networks. Plus, you can create products, like a special report, and give them away as enticements for readers to join your mailing list or subscribe to your blog. Thus your information products become promotional tools as well.

CREATE RELATED INFORMATION PRODUCTS FOR MULTIPLE STREAMS OF INCOME

Information products provide consumers with the information they need or want, solve problems, offer expert advice, educate, or in some way provide a service, tip, or tool. The information is packaged in a variety of ways and sold, usually on the Internet, which makes your blog or website a great place to promote them.

Your blog itself is a treasure trove of information. You can turn the jewels there—in this case, posts—into products, such as special reports, videos, recordings (MP3s, CDs, or DVDs), e-books, workbooks, teleseminars, webinars, home study courses, online courses, or even books—all based on blog posts. When you finish blogging your book—or even while you are blogging your book (or if you have simply been blogging with no thought until now of a book), information products can provide you with great income sources.

Your blogged, printed, or e-book shouldn't be your only source of income; if it is, you might find yourself earning less than you might like. Instead, use your blogged book to create multiple streams of income.

Here's how you start: First, you will need a mechanism for selling your information products. You can create a page on your blog site or on your website with a shopping cart system so readers or visitors can purchase these items any time, day or night, by downloading them. You may want to sign up for a service like 1ShoppingCart.com so an auto-responder sends the purchased items immediately, or simply use PayPal.com and send them out manually. There are ways to hook up PayPal.com with mailing list services, like AWeber.com, and use their autoresponders to send out products, but it's a bit more complicated.

Second, look at your manuscript and see what parts of it could be expanded:

- What blogged book posts might be subjects of their own?
- What topics could be expanded into another series of posts?
- What topics have you blogged about that generated a lot of interest from your readers in the form of comments or queries?
- What topic did you want to cover but it just didn't fit into the scheme of your blogged book or of a particular chapter?

The answers to these questions all might generate good information products.

Third, look at your manuscript for topics you already have covered as a series of posts. Maybe you wrote five posts on a particular topic that lends itself to a special report or to a course of some sort. Do your readers want to learn how to do whatever you were writing about? If so, this could work as a product.

TYPES OF INFORMATION PRODUCTS TO CREATE

What types of information products might you create? Here's a quick list:

1. TIP SHEETS OR BOOKS OR BOOKLETS: Do you offer a lot of tips on your blog? Do you have a lot of great advice in the posts of your blogged book? Pull these out into a tip sheet or a tip book. These short books consist solely of tips—just a list of great advice in little snippets. Include twenty tips on a page that you then convert into a PDF: thirty days' worth of tips or one hundred tips that you turn into a short book or booklet. If you have a bit more to say, consider producing a tip booklet that offers one tip per page with a little bit of copy explaining the tip. You can publish them inexpensively as a PDF, an e-book, or as a printed and saddle-stitched (stapled) booklet.

You may be able to produce other kinds of booklets based on your blog copy as well. If you can find a printer with a booklet press, these will cost you just dollars to produce. All you do is send off a PDF, and voilà! You have a booklet. Like POD, you can print one or one thousand. A short book (sixty pages or less) can be produced inexpensively on a booklet press in most cases. Depending upon page count, in some cases you might also be able to produce these as POD books.

2. SPECIAL REPORTS: You can produce a special report on almost anything. These are short, informative documents, usually under ten pages, on one highly focused topic. Often they are written for professionals. For example, I created one on how to build author platform; I sell it for $10, and I give it away to those who sign up for my mailing list. I created it out of a number of blog posts I edited together, along with a little extra copy to flesh it out.

Look at your blogged book or your blog, and consider what content might lend itself to a special report. What do your readers want or need to know? What problem can you solve for them? What could you tell them in a few short pages? Maybe something interesting or new or newsworthy has happened that relates to your blogged book; this could be additional content you could use for a special report as well, and then you could promote your blogged book (or blog) by publicizing the report for sale at your blogged book site.

3. VIDEOS AND RECORDINGS: I mentioned videos and how to create them for YouTube in chapter seven. You also can create educational videos and sell them. The same goes for recordings. Plus, I highly recommend you videotape or record almost anything you do—teleseminars, workshops, speeches, radio interviews. You can then sell them or use them in some other way as information products.

Creating audio recordings is simple. Purchase a decent digital recorder, record yourself reading blog posts, talking about your blogged book, or telling people how to do different things related to the topic of your blogged book. Sell these as products—MP3s for iPods and such. Or put them on CDs. (You also can upload them on blog posts so people can listen to them, and you can then let them know that more such audio recordings are available for sale.) Most digital recorders come with instructions for uploading the audio files and converting them from WAV files to MP3s and such. Plus, there are easy audio editing programs available online, such as Audacity.

4. HOME STUDY AND ONLINE COURSES: If your book lends itself to you teaching others how to do something, consider combining some of your blog posts or special reports with your audio and video to create home study or online courses. Or take some of your blogged book or blog material and create a workbook that you combine with audio and video. You can do this without the audio and video as well, or you can just use a printed workbook or some sort of online program you facilitate. You also can combine this with teleseminars, workshops, or coaching. People will pay a lot of money for such products.

5. COACHING AND CONSULTING: If your blogged book or blog offers great information that teaches people about how to do something, consider providing coaching and consulting services. Advertise them on your blog or website. (By the way, if you want to do this, get that printed book out right away. There's nothing that will give you more credibility as an expert than becoming the author of a printed book.)

6. BOOKS: We've already spoken a great deal about books. You can go back to chapter eight to learn all about turning your blogged book into a printed book. Here I'd like to discuss one facet of turning blogs into books: booking a blog. If you recall, booking a blog means repurposing your blog posts into a book when you didn't plan on blogging a book from the start. So, for those bloggers who might not have planned on writing a book but find themselves with a year or more of great content and want to turn it into a book, you can book your blog (as opposed to blogging your book).

This entails going through your blog and pulling out all the posts you feel should be in your book. Here's how you start: Create a table of contents and synopsize your chapters. Then go through your blog categories looking for the content (posts) that fits into your chapters. You can also search using the tags you created. (Tags are the keywords, or search terms, you used in your blog posts that you listed in the "tags" area prior to publishing your posts.) Copy and paste these posts into a Word document, chapter by chapter, thus creating a manuscript. Create subheads if you need them, but your blog post titles should suffice.

You also can look at your blog archive and search for strong themes that work together or topics you've covered often or in depth. Pull these out and see if you can mold a book around them. If so, build a table of contents around this initial content and then go back through your archives looking for additional posts that might flesh out the book.

In either case, you will need to write additional copy, edit, and revise as suggested in chapter eight of this book. You could then create both an e-book and a printed book, and sell it from your blog website, Smashwords.com, and from Amazon.com.

Don't forget that you can always excerpt material from your blogged book as a giveaway if you package it as something new and interesting. Add a video or audio element to it and offer it as an enticement to mailing list subscribers. Also, every time you offer a teleseminar or a recording, you can ask for an "opt in" to your mailing list.

I failed miserably at getting people to subscribe to my blog and mailing list. Don't make that mistake. You want subscribers as well as readers. You want to know people love what you are doing enough to actually want to hear from you. So, use all these information products as tools in your toolbox to draw those readers into your subscriber list. Then you can sell these products to them from that list as well. Mailing lists are extremely important. If social networks for some reason fail to be important, or crash and burn, your mailing list will still be there.

All these products will work for you night and day, 24/7, if you set up a great storefront in cyberspace. That's the beauty of a blog and information products working together. You can create that dream of money going into the bank while you sleep, and it won't just be from your books. And here's the great thing: The more people come to use and to love all your products and services, the more people will buy your book.

CHAPTER 10:

BLOG-TO-BOOK SUCCESS STORIES

If you want to learn how to succeed at anything in life, ask those who have already achieved success how they did so. Create a road map out of their success stories. Ask them for tips and advice. Allow them to mentor you, even if only via their willingness to answer your questions. Then model them as best you can in your own unique way.

When it comes to blogging a book, there aren't too many people who have set out to actually write a book from start to finish using blog technology. Thus I cannot look at actual blogged-book success stories or ask successful book bloggers to tell you how they achieved their success. However, I can report back on some of the bloggers who landed book deals—the blog-to-book success stories we all have heard so much about—and ask how one might achieve similar success.

In this chapter you'll hear directly from five bloggers who indeed landed blog-to-book deals. All five have had tremendous success with their blogs and, subsequently, with their books as well. Read on and learn.

PAMELA SLIM ON GOING FROM BLOG TO BOOK: *ESCAPE FROM CUBICLE NATION*

Pamela Slim's Escape from Cubicle Nation blog, which can be found at www.escapefromcubiclenation.com/pamela-slims-blog, provides support, resources, information, and training for corporate employees who aspire to start their own businesses. She started the blog in October of 2005, and it was later tapped for a book by the same name by Penguin/Portfolio. *Escape from Cubicle Nation: From Corporate Prisoner to Thriving Entrepreneur,* which was released in 2009 and contains about 70 percent new content and 30 percent blog posts. Because she wrote a how-to book for readers, Slim says, "There was lots of context I had to wrap around the individual posts that illustrated particular points."

1. Why did you begin blogging?

I started blogging for the specific purpose of building an online presence and a client base for my business coaching practice. Prior to starting my blog, I had been a successful consultant to large corporations for ten years, marketing my business primarily with word-of-mouth referrals. I moved to Arizona from the San Francisco Bay Area and got married. Because we knew we wanted to have children, I wanted to shift my business model from in-person consulting, which involved lots of travel, to online coaching and writing. I started my blog when my son was seven months old.

2. How did you choose your topic?

As a consultant, I worked with thousands of employees and executives from every type of business you could imagine. In every company, regardless of its reputation or financial situation, there were always a few people who would pull me aside and quietly say, "I would love to work for myself, but I have no idea how to do it! Can you help me?" It was always curious to me that they felt starting a business was such a mystery since there were thousands of books and blogs on the subject.

After researching the topic and getting trained by Martha Beck as a life coach, it became clear to me that, while there was tons of information about starting a business, there were very few resources that integrated the stress of personal change with the business journey itself. So I decided to write about the things I knew were on people's minds but that they would probably never admit in public: like how you can get over the fear of telling your spouse you want to quit your job to start a business, or how you can avoid living in a van down by the river if your business plans go awry.

3. What, if any, market research did you do before beginning your blog?

I did a fair amount of work researching the demographics and psychographics of my target audience by describing their profile in detail and doing lots of keyword searches on terms like "start a business" and "become an entrepreneur" to see what kinds of resources were available. I also looked up lots of popular blogs on Technorati, the most robust directory at the time, to see what best-in-class blogs looked like. Beyond that, I did not do tons of research, since I was passionate about the topic and convinced there was a market for what I wanted to write about.

4. Did you think you were writing a book, did you plan on blogging a book, or were you simply blogging on your topic? (In retrospect, would doing one or the other have made it easier to later write your book?)

I had no intention of writing a book when I first started my blog. I was writing it to grow my business and to create a body of good online content, so I was quite surprised when publishers began expressing interest in a book. If I had known beforehand that I was working on a book, I think it would have tripped me up because I may have approached it from a more structured perspective instead of writing only about things that I felt passionate about.

5. How long did it take for you to gain blog readers, and can you pinpoint any certain event that created a tipping point when readership increased noticeably?

It took about a year to develop a steady group of readers. It was very slow at first, but I found great joy in writing so I kept producing posts.

One big tipping point for me was getting featured on venture capitalist and author Guy Kawasaki's blog in May of 2006. He was extremely influential in my target market. When he featured my post "An Open Letter to CEOs Across the Corporate World" on his blog (www.escapefromcubi-clenation.com/2006/05/04/open-letter-to-ceos-coos-cios-and-cfos-across-the-corporate-world/), traffic and subscribers exploded. After that exposure, my growth was quicker and supported by influencers like Seth Godin, Kathy Sierra, and Hugh MacLeod.

6. What did you do to drive traffic (readers) to your blog?

My best strategy for drawing traffic to the bog was to continually turn out relevant content for my market. Without this, I don't think I would have the long-standing support I enjoy today. I also frequently wrote about other authors and bloggers, which led to mutual support, friendship, and connection.

When Twitter and Facebook came on the scene, they helped amplify individual posts and increase my reader base.

Due to the topic of my blog, I got quoted quite a bit in mainstream press like *The New York Times*, *BusinessWeek*, *Fortune*, *Psychology Today*, and *USA Today*. This helped to increase my blog's visibility and cement the credibility of my message.

7. How did your blog-to-book deal come about?

An author friend introduced me to his agent and suggested we work together to outline a book. I worked with the agent for a few months, but we never really gelled; I didn't feel passionate about the outline we had created for the book. I blogged about the experience and told my readers I was going to step back from pursuing a book deal for awhile to focus on writing more on my blog.

About a year later, I got an e-mail from Emily Rapoport, an editor at Penguin, who said, "I read on your blog that you were interested in writing a book. Could we talk about it?" Needless to say, I jumped at the chance, and we started brainstorming ideas. I felt immediate rapport with her, so she introduced me to an agent she had worked with, and we put together a proposal in about three weeks. We turned it in on a Friday and by Tuesday had a signed deal. We had a fantastic working relationship the whole way through the project, so it was especially sweet when our book won Best Small Business/Entrepreneur Book of 2009 from 800 CEO Read.

8. What advice would you give writers who want to blog a book (and build readership/platform while doing so)?

The best place to try out ideas for a book is on a blog! Don't let yourself get stressed out by book structure or perfect writing. Pay attention to the kinds of things your readers are interested in and experiment often. You will need many more times raw content from your blog than you can fit in your book, so write with abandon.

9. What's the most important thing a blogger can do to get noticed in the blogosphere?

Write great stuff. In an ever-increasing sea of content, only the really great blogs will get noticed. People will not be passionate about sharing mediocre writing.

Stay humble. Promote other great writers frequently—not to cultivate favors, but because you feel that what they have to say will help your readers. Generosity, sharing, and fostering great work will always beat short-term political posturing.

REGGIE SOLOMON ON GOING FROM BLOG TO BOOK: *I GARDEN URBAN STYLE*

Reggie Solomon is the creator of two blogs, UrbanGardenCasual.com and TomatoCasual.com. UrbanGardenCasual.com is focused on helping urban dweller's garden, and TomatoCasual.com is focused on everything tomato for people who love tomatoes.

His book, *I Garden Urban Style*, produced with co-author Michael Nolan, is based on his blog UrbanGardenCasual.com. The book arms readers with the knowledge they need to get the most satisfying results from their urban gardening efforts and investment. The book offers instruction on many urban gardening options, from window gardens to container gardens to herb gardens to community gardens, appealing to a wide variety of people from those wanting to commit little time and effort to those wanting an active, fulfilling hobby. The book closely resembles the blog but has striking and vivid photography. "We even included article pullouts directly from the blog in the book," says Solomon. "This book definitely feels like my blog, but richer."

1. Why did you begin blogging?

I began blogging in 2007 as an experiment in engaging emerging media and new ways of working using the Internet. Through the experience of blogging, I learned how to hire people virtually, manage and work with remote teams around the world, and build a customized blog interface without having any technical knowledge, all while assembling specialized knowledge on a couple of niche subjects of interest. Not bad for a side project. Two years after starting my blog, I landed my first book deal.

2. How did you choose your topic?

Niche is the new black, and so went the subjects covered on my blogs, Tomato Casual and Urban Garden Casual.

I chose these two niche areas in part because no one else was blogging about them. I began with the goal to assemble the world's largest repository of articles about tomatoes and urban gardening, and, especially with the case of tomatoes, I've pretty much done it. I knew that if I could create the most content on these two specialized subjects, the Internet would lead readers to my door, and I could eventually figure out a way to monetize that interest. Producing a book is one of the ways I'm doing that, and I expect other opportunities to emerge in the future.

TomatoCasual.com is focused on "Everything Tomato for People who Love Tomatoes." We are not only obsessed with growing, eating, and cooking with tomatoes, we're also obsessed with all things tomato whether it be art, music, wallpaper, recipes, or movies. We are passionate about tomatoes.

UrbanGardenCasual.com is focused on "Gardening for the Urban Dweller." We help city dwellers reclaim the pleasures of non-city living within the confines of urban space by bridging traditional gardening with the special needs of urban and small-space gardeners in the modern world. We want to help people be as comfortable gardening as they are shuffling between tracks on their iPods.

With both blogs, I chose to engage my niches with a decidedly "casual" take and built "casual" into the actual branding. We have taken what has largely been written about from a dry and technical perspective and have made it our own by making it casual and thus more accessible.

3. What, if any, market research did you do before beginning your blog?

A personal interest in growing tomatoes and gardening in the city served as the primary motivation behind the creation of both blogs; however, I did qualify both interests to ensure there was a market for information on both topics.

What's the most popular item grown in an American garden? What item do you find on the cover of most seed magazines and popularly sold at big-box home improvement stores and gardening centers? What item can be inexpensively grown in one's own garden with a taste far superior to that found in stores at premium prices? Yep. Tomatoes!

In the case of urban gardening, I couldn't find any resources that addressed the particular urban gardening interest. Most of the books I read focused on high-end landscaping of small urban spaces, but there were few resources for gardeners like me who were focused on affordable small-space vegetable gardening. I wanted to live more sustainably and reduce my carbon imprint. This growing trend combined with being a foodie who prizes fresh ingredients made my focus on urban gardening seem market ready.

4. Did you think you were writing a book, did you plan on blogging a book, or were you simply blogging on your topic? (In retrospect, would doing one or the other have made it easier to later write your book?)

I outsource most of the content creation of my blogs. It became apparent very quickly after trying to produce content for both blogs myself that my bigger competitive advantage would be in assembling the most information about both niche areas rather than making the blogs solely about my personal perspective and voice. I have two to five writers working for me at any time who create most of the content for my sites.

While I did not begin blogging with the explicit plan to write a book, it did pass my mind from time to time. It was not until a niche hobby-book publisher approached me and asked me if I would be interested in writing a book on urban gardening and submitting a book proposal for their review that I seriously moved the idea from dinner party chatter to action.

Again, my goal when I started both blogs was to assemble the world's largest collection of information on tomatoes and urban gardening and respond to whatever opportunities this brought to my door. The fact that my urban garden blog pops up within the first three results on Google for "urban garden" searches did not go unnoticed by my publisher and is likely how they found me. My blog is a top destination for reaching and marketing to urban gardeners. What better platform from which to launch a niche book?

5. How long did it take for you to gain blog readers, and can you pinpoint any certain event that created a tipping point when readership increased noticeably?

It took me about two years to build an audience for both blogs. Engaging social networking definitely helped. I opened groups on Flickr.com for people to share photos of their urban gardening and tomato adventures and honestly forgot about the group I'd set up. I was utterly surprised in checking my Flickr page a year later to find hundreds of people were submitting photos to my groups regularly. A similar occurrence happened after setting up my Facebook and Twitter pages as well.

I've considered outsourcing the social networking management of my site, since I know this could be done better. We may all wish for a silver bullet to bolster readership, but it's less a case of scoring a home run and more a case of getting singles on the board. Google PageRank rewards this latter strategy, too.

6. What did you do to drive traffic (readers) to your blog?

I equipped my sites with tools to help people share content with friends. I've always had buttons that have made it easy to send articles to friends and to share content within popular social networks. Producing good content and hiring enthusiastic writers for my blogs who have communities in which they share content also helped drive traffic to my sites. My blogs have been featured in *The New York Times* and *Fox TV News,* and they have been linked to many other popular periodicals, websites, and publications.

7. What one or two things that you did would you attribute to your blogging success (and to the book deal you landed)?

Niche focus has been the key to my blogging success. My blogs would not enjoy the traction they do if I didn't serve up fresh, focused content to feed hungry search engines. Having an enthusiastic and talented group of writers and contributors has also been key to the success of my blogs and book. I partnered with one of my writers, Michael Nolan, to produce the book, and we featured the work of many of my other blog contributors. I'm happy the publishing of the book helped my entire writing team become published authors and contributors. The blog has been a product of "we" from the beginning, and so has the book. "We" is how I roll.

8. What advice would you give to writers who want to blog a book (and build readership/platform while doing so)?

Focus on building quality content. It will be the foundation of your success.

We publish two to three times a week with posts averaging 250 to 500 words. When we occasionally have articles that are longer, we break them up into Part 1 and Part 2 articles. Google eats fresh content for breakfast, lunch, and dinner, so spread out your content as you do your meals. You wouldn't eat all of your food for the week on Monday and not expect to get hungry during the week. The same goes for Google. Feed it and wean it to whatever posting frequency makes sense for you; just be consistent with your publishing schedule so your readers know what to expect.

Building readership is about relationship building. Build relationships through your blog as you would in person. We reached out to many of our early readers and mentioned them in our blog and visited their blogs to comment. It's all about relationships—so easy to build and sometimes easier to squander.

Lastly, think carefully if you want to be published through a traditional publishing channel. Having one's book published through a traditional publisher does earn one a bit of cred, but consider whether long-term earnings from e-book publishing might be more attractive. Self-publishing through an e-book format may prove the most profitable in the long run while giving you maximum control over your creative content.

9. What's the most important thing a blogger can do to get noticed in the blogosphere?

To get noticed, be noticeable. Not by SEO gaming tricks but by producing content that attracts positive attention to itself. Big-media shouts; niche media whispers. The long-tail (ala Chris Anderson*) belongs to whisperers. Lucky we merry band of whisperers.

[* Chris Anderson is editor in chief of *Wired*. He wrote an article in the magazine titled "The Long Tail," which he expanded upon in the book *The Long Tail: Why the Future of Business Is Selling Less of More*.]

Also, write more about the topics people come to your blog to find information on. Using a backend blog analytics package, such as Google Analytics or Performancing Metrics, you can easily find the search terms leading people to your site and create more content for users looking for information about that subject or concept. This means you can produce content just as easily from Z to A as you can from A to Z.

And lastly, have fun with it!

BRETT McKAY ON GOING FROM BLOG TO BOOK: *THE ART OF MANLINESS*

Theartofmanliness.com is a 100,000 + subscriber blog started in 2008 by Brett McKay and his wife Kate. According to Brett McKay, the blog is dedicated to "reviving the lost art of manliness" and publishes articles on things like self-improvement, relationships, dressing and grooming, etiquette, health, finance, and "manly" skills. The goal of the site is to help men better themselves in all areas of their lives.

Based on the blog, the book *The Art of Manliness: Classic Skills and Manners for the Modern Man,* was published in October 2009 by HOW Books. Seventy-five percent of the book consists of articles taken from the blog and edited for the book, and 25 percent of the book's content is new material.

1. Why did you begin blogging?

I began blogging as a hobby in 2006 during my first year of law school. My first blog was called The Frugal Law Student (Frugallawstudent.com), and the focus was on personal finance for those in law school. I had some mild success with it. In 2008, I started Theartofmanliness.com.

2. How did you choose your topic?

I was tired of the content geared toward men in magazines like *Men's Health* and *GQ.* It was always about the same stuff—six-pack abs, getting chicks, and expensive clothes. Theartofmanliness.com is the men's magazine I've always wanted to read. At the same time, it seemed like twenty-something guys like me were a little adrift and had lost some of the basic skills and knowledge our grandpas knew. I wanted to rediscover the lost manly arts.

3. What, if any, market research did you do before beginning your blog?

I didn't do any market research. I just wrote about topics that interested me and discovered that lots of other men were interested in the same stuff as well.

4. Did you think you were writing a book, did you plan on blogging a book, or were you simply blogging on your topic? (In retrospect, would doing one or the other have made it easier to later write your book?)

I didn't think I was writing a book when I started Theartofmanliness.com. I was simply blogging about my topic. When we started getting more traffic and things picked up, I started to think, "Hey, maybe we can turn this thing into a book."

5. How long did it take for you to gain blog readers, and can you pinpoint any certain event that created a tipping point when readership increased noticeably?

The site took off fairly quickly after I started it. The very first post I wrote, "How to Shave Like Your Grandpa," got picked up on Digg.com and reddit.com, which brought in a ton of traffic. (This was back when getting on the front page of Digg was a huge deal).

6. What did you do to drive traffic (readers) to your blog?

First, I leveraged the audience I already had built up at frugallawstudent.com. Right off the bat in the first month of Theartofmanliness.com I was able to score five hundred subscribers.

And then again, the big thing that rocketed our blog to success was getting discovered on social media sites like Digg.com, Delicious.com, and reddit.com. Every week or so one of our posts would hit the front page of those sites and send tens of thousands of visitors to our site in just a few hours. Other big websites would spot our links on Digg or reddit, link to us, and send more traffic our way. In just five months after starting the blog, we had over ten thousand subscribers.

7. How did your blog-to-book deal come about?

We actually didn't pitch our book or come up with a book proposal. About five months after we started Theartofmanliness.com, several editors from different publishers e-mailed us wanting to turn our blog into a book. We took a look at the different offers and decided to go with HOW Books. We inked the deal in July 2008 and started on the draft in August 2008. We turned in the completed book in December 2008, and the book was published in October 2009.

8. What one or two things that you did would you attribute to your blogging success (and to the book deal you landed)?

Identifying an untapped niche was probably the most important thing. There wasn't a magazine out there that appealed to the thousands of men who weren't interested in hot babes and cars and earnestly wanted to learn how to improve their lives and become better men, men who were interested in good, old-fashioned, wholesome manliness. We found success by filling that void.

9. What advice would you give writers who wanted to blog a book (and build readership/platform while doing so)?

Create a blog that stands out from the thousands of others out there, and work hard to make it popular. Showing publishers you have a big following will make getting a book deal far easier.

10. What's the most important thing a blogger can do to get noticed in the blogosphere?

I know it's cliche, but writing interesting, unique, helpful, top-quality content is the key—"evergreen" content that will be just as useful to people five years from now. We set ourselves apart from other sites in that we don't just look at other blogs to get ideas and regurgitate what is already being shared around the Web. Instead, we do a ton of research—we check out lots of books from the library and spend hours poring through them.

Besides quality content-creation, be helpful to people in the blogosphere. Link to them on your blog, share their links on Twitter and Face-

http://howtoblogabook.com

book, and e-mail them with tips for their own blog. Don't just focus on the big fish either. Focus on the small guys, too.

MARTHA ALDERSON ON GOING FROM BLOG TO BOOK: *THE PLOT WHISPERER*

Martha Alderson uses her blog, The Plot Whisperer (http://plotwhisperer. blogspot.com), as a place for her to unwind after plot consultations with clients and to share plot tips. "Because writing is a very personal activity (as well as a very public activity—after all, a writer's intention is to be read), a certain intimacy forms between my clients and me during plot consultations," she explains. "As a result, I've been able to draw lessons about how stories unfold and to include the lives of the writers with whom I work in my blog."

The Plot Whisperer: Secrets of Story Structure Any Writer Can Master organizes Alderson's blog posts into the ultimate guide to writing page-turning novels, memoirs, and screenplays that sell. It was released by Adams Media in October 2011. Although the rough draft of the book was about 90 percent from the blog, Alderson says, "In the editing process, things shifted and changed so that, though the blog is reflected throughout the book, probably 40 percent is from the blog and 60 percent is new content."

1. Why did you begin blogging?

I began teaching plot to writers when writers' websites were still a rarity and mostly static. When blogs came along, I loved how easy it was to offer updated information, receive nearly instantaneous feedback, and remain interactive with visitors.

2. How did you choose your topic?

I hang up the phone or turn off Skype after a plot consultation and invariably continue to mull over insights I gleaned and impressions I was struck with. Often, relevant information bubbles to the surface and rather than allow the insight or feedback or wisdom to languish, I choose instead to share on my blog what I learn with and from other writers.

3. What, if any, market research did you do before beginning your blog?

It never even occurred to me to do market research.

4. Did you think you were writing a book, did you plan on blogging a book, or were you simply blogging on your topic?

I was simply blogging about plot.

5. How long did it take for you to gain blog readers, and can you pinpoint any certain event that created a tipping point when readership increased noticeably?

As soon as other writers started blogging about the help I provided them through my first book, *Blockbuster Plots Pure & Simple*, plot consultations, conferences, workshops, and retreats, my readership began growing. Writer's blogs and websites bigger than mine, like The Daily Coyote, The Writers Store, and NaNoWriMo (National Novel Writing Month), started linking to my website and continue to send writers to the Plot Whisperer blog today. *Writer's Digest* magazine awarded the Plot Whisperer blog the honor of a spot as one of the 101 Best Websites for Writers for three years running and directs new visitors to the blog each year.

6. What did you do to drive traffic (readers) to your blog?

I use my website, Blockbuster Plots for Writers, as well as Facebook, Twitter, LinkedIn, Goodreads, and my blog, How Do I Plot a Novel, Memoir, Screenplay?

I strive monthly to send out a free plot tips e-zine to subscribers and pack it with plot support. The e-zine always has a link to the most recent blog post and is a terrific way to stay in touch with writers who know me or know of my work.

I find different demographics prefer different modes of keeping in touch; thus I attempt to cast out the broadest reach I can—using Twitter,

YouTube, my blog, my website, and Facebook to send out plot tips, inspiration, and support to writers all over the world.

7. How did your blog-to-book deal come about?

My agent was pitching a second edition of *Blockbuster Plots Pure & Simple* and instead Paula Munier, acquisitions editor for Adams Media, asked me to write *The Plot Whisperer* book based on my blog.

8. What one or two things that you did would you attribute to your blogging success (and to the book deal you landed)?

My deepest intention always has been to share useful information with writers. Writing a story from beginning to end is no easy feat. I wish to help other writers achieve their dreams of completing a worthy project. During a plot consultation, I try to reawaken in writers the rhythm of the Universal Story form. Stories reflect the heartbeat of the universe. Writers and readers, all of us, pulse to this universal rhythm. I think the exploration of universal truths through my blog inspires writers—and blog readers.

9. What advice would you give writers who wanted to blog a book (and build readership/platform while doing so)?

Write your passion. Always consider your visitors. Update your blog consistently.

10. What's the most important thing a blogger can do to get noticed in the blogosphere?

Share valuable information that is true and authentic to you.

CHRISTIAN LANDER ON GOING FROM BLOG TO BOOK: *STUFF WHITE PEOPLE LIKE*

Christian Lander reportedly received a $350,000 advance from Random House Trade Paperbacks to turn his blog, Stuffwhitepeoplelike.com, into a book, *Stuff*

White People Like, The Definitive Guide to the Unique Taste of Millions. Lander says, "The blog and the book are both a comedic guide to white people." The book consists of 50 percent new material including charts, graphs, and other work from graphic designers.

1. Why did you begin blogging?

I started blogging to entertain my friends. I have a group of buddies who I think are hilarious, and we are always trying to make each other laugh. Since I can't be in the same city as them, I found that writing was a fun way to keep them entertained. There isn't really anything in the world I enjoy more than making people laugh.

2. How did you choose your topic?

My friend Myles and I were talking about the TV show *The Wire*, and Myles said he didn't trust any white person who didn't watch the show. So we started guessing what these people were doing instead of watching *The Wire*, and we came up with things like yoga, getting divorced, and having gifted kids. Then I said, "It's blog time," and started writing to make him laugh.

3. What, if any, market research did you do before beginning your blog?

Absolutely nothing. I started the blog to make my friends laugh; all of the success has been a by-product.

4. Did you think you were writing a book, did you plan on blogging a book, or were you simply blogging on your topic?

I was blogging only to make my friends laugh. I had no idea the blog could become a book, and this was back in 2008 when publishing had really cooled off on blog-to-book deals.

5. How long did it take for you to gain blog readers, and can you pinpoint any certain event that created a tipping point when readership increased noticeably?

It took about three weeks to go from 100 hits a day to 30,000 hits a day. From there it blew up to hundreds of thousands of hits. The day it exploded was the day it was featured on Comedy Central's *Insider*. Truthfully, the traffic from major media outlets was nice, but sites like StumbleUpon.com always added more traffic than any traditional media source. So while big media can start the spark, it's people sharing the posts over social media that causes a blog to really grow.

6. What did you do to drive traffic (readers) to your blog?

I kept writing. I know that sounds obnoxious, but it's true. I didn't try to change anything. I figured I was successful because I offered people a laugh, and so trying to do anything to change that seemed foolish. Also, I agreed to do every single interview request that came through the site: blogs, student papers, podcasts, all of it.

7. How did your blog-to-book deal come about?

The site became very, very popular, and literary agents started contacting me. That was it.

8. What one or two things that you did would you attribute to your blogging success (and to the book deal you landed)?

Luck. Luck more than anything. The truth is that success is only partially merit based. I was lucky enough to write on a topic that came along at exactly the right time in terms of publishing, the Internet, and America's willingness to think about race and class.

Also, I think that people could see I was writing because I loved it and that the blog wasn't set up to try to make the readers do all the work. What I mean by that is a lot people write blogs and then expect their friends and readers to share them with everyone and do the work of promotion. The truth is that if your blog is good enough and connects with enough people, they will share it on their own. You can't have your readers do your work for you. You have to make it so good and so compelling that readers have no choice but to forward it on.

9. What advice would you give writers wanting to blog a book (and build readership/platform while doing so)?

Don't do it. Blog because you love it. Blog because you're a writer who needs to exercise his ability to write. Do not go into this with dollar signs in your eyes or else everyone who reads your blog will see right through you.

Also, when it comes to readers and comments, do not take the negative ones personally. Do your best to ignore them; the energy required to convert someone who already dislikes you is not repaid. Just accept that no one is liked by everyone, and embrace the people who like what you do.

10. What's the most important thing a blogger can do to get noticed in the blogosphere?

Be good, and remember that success is not a sign of your skill as a writer. If John Milton had a blog today no one would read it. Success is based partially on talent, but mostly on an ability to connect with a broad audience. So when it comes to getting noticed you have to have an original idea you execute well.

Also the "Hollywood system" is a good one for blogging. Can you tell me what your blog is about in a sentence? If you can't, it probably isn't going to be broadly popular.

CONCLUSION:

HOW THE *HOW TO BLOG A BOOK* BLOG GOT PUBLISHED

I began the *How to Blog a Book* blog in February 2009. I completed the whole book before the end of June 2010—just five months later.

So, what happened to the blogged book when I finished? At first I blogged sporadically, relieved to be done with that first draft. I began posting blogs to *How to Blog a Book* just when I thought of it, maybe once a week, a few times a month, when I saw a blog-to-book success story or I heard a bit of interesting blogging or publishing news. I didn't want to let the blog die, but I also did not want to devote a ton of time to it. I had four other blogs that needed my attention after all.

In September, I began working on a proposal. As soon as my agent heard I had finished blogging the book, she encouraged me to send her one so she could start marketing the book. In mid-November, I sent her a final version, which she submitted to several publishers. We revised the *How to Blog a Book* proposal in January and again in February 2011 after receiving a few rejections. She then sent it to Writer's Digest Books. In March we revised the proposal once more and re-sent it to Writer's Digest—to the same acquisitions editor, whom we had not heard from yet.

During this time, I kept reiterating to my agent that I wanted to get the book out quickly. I wanted to be first to market with the idea. I told her I would self-publish if need be, and I began editing the manuscript and thinking about a design for the book's cover.

In early July I heard the good news that the acquisitions editor and the publisher had accepted the book—if I would agree to write 10,000 words more than I proposed. I, of course, agreed. (I'm a very verbose writer. Writing too little is never a problem for me.) I was told the proposal would be presented to the sales and marketing team just a week or two later. So we waited again … a few days past that date of that meeting. Then my agent got the call that the book had been accepted. Woo-hoo!

However, since Writer's Digest Books also wanted to be first to market, I was given a deadline just eight weeks out from the time the book was accepted. I was planning to be away one of those weeks at a conference, and three and a half of the weeks I would be in New York City with my son. I'd be working, but only for a few hours per day. That meant I had three weeks to get the manuscript edited and revised and make any additions, including the two chapters that weren't written. Additionally, one of the chapters involved inviting contributors to participate, and if they didn't agree, I might not meet my deadline. I had my work cut out for me.

When I received the actual contract two weeks after I returned home, the deadlines had changed. I had to turn in just one quarter of the manuscript before I left for New York, and I had two more months to turn in the rest. Too late. As I put my signature on the contract, I'd already completed all of the book except the chapter that required contributors. This I would turn in when I returned from New York about a month and half later.

Just seven months after turning in the final chapter, I held a bound and printed copy of *How to Blog a Book* in my hands—proof that the concept presented in my blogged book really does work. If you take a great idea, produce and carry out a strong business plan, build a great platform on the Internet by blogging your book and driving traffic to that blog, you can land a traditional publishing deal.

If I can do it, so can you.

There's no time like now to be a writer, a blogger, or an author. The publishing industry is an exciting place to hang your hats—your business person's and your writer's hats, your publisher's and your blogger's hats. But don't just hang them up. Put them on! Do the work and get your book blogged and published. I hope you will sit down at your computer and start blogging your book (if you haven't already).

Here's my challenge to you: Blog a book in a year or less. How? Easy. A blog post a day is a book—or two—a year. Think about it: Three hundred and sixty posts times 250 words equals 90,000 words. That's easily two short nonfiction books or one long novel. I challenge you to begin writing a blog post a day and to set a goal to finish blogging a book in a year ... or less—and, of course, to get discovered (or at least published) in the process.

Good luck!

ABOUT THE AUTHOR

Nina Amir, Your Inspiration-to-Creation Coach, inspires writers to create the results they desire—publishable and published products and careers as writers and authors. Nina inspires people to combine their purpose and their passion so they Achieve More Inspired Results.

Nina is a nonfiction editor, book proposal consultant, and writing, book, blogging, and author coach with more than 33 years of experience in the publishing field. She offers these services through her company, CopyWright Communications. Nina also is the founder of *Write Nonfiction in November*, a yearly writing challenge accompanied by a blog. She writes four other blogs, including *Write Nonfiction NOW!* and *How to Blog a Book*, two national columns at Examiner.com, and her blogs can be found on Redroom.com and VibrantNation.com. She is the weekly writing and publishing expert on Michael Ray Dresser's popular radio show, *Dresser After Dark*.

Nina holds a B.A. in magazine journalism from Syracuse University, with a concentration in psychology. She is a certified life coach and rebirther and is trained as a Voice Dialogue facilitator.

Nina has edited or written for more than 45 magazines, newspapers, e-zines, and newsletters on a full-time or freelance basis producing hundreds of articles. Her essays have been published in five anthologies and can be found in numerous e-zines and Internet article directories, and she has self-published nine short books, including *How to Evaluate Your Book For Success*.

Currently, Nina lives in the Santa Cruz Mountains in Northern California with her husband. She has two children who no longer live at home.

www.ninaamir.com
www.copywrightcommunications.com

http://howtoblogabook.com

INDEX

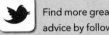